GW01511166

The goal of Friends of the […] reader with examples of rol[…] walks of life, backgrounds, […]ntries, and were not maʿṣūm. It is to encourage and reassure the reader of their capabilities and potential. The stories in this compilation were hand picked with practical lessons that we can implement—lessons on kindness, love for education, striving for hard work, etc. If these ordinary individuals could accomplish such a high status and grow so close to the Imāms of their times, surely we can do the same, and get close to our hidden Imām. We pray that through these engaging stories, the reader connects with the Ahl al-Bayt and their companions and emulates the teachings of our truest role models.

We hope that you and your children enjoy these books and use them as a means to achieve this goal, inshāʾAllāh.

We pray to Allah to give us the strength and tawfīq to perform our duties and responsibilities.

With Duʿās,

Nabi R. Mir (Abidi)

Table of Contents

Chapter 13. City of Knowledge

Zakariyyā ibn Ādam

page *163*

Chapter 14. The Imām's Defender

Abū aṣ-Ṣalt

page *173*

Chapter 15. Searching for Light

Ḥasan ibn Saʿīd

page *191*

Chapter 16. The Poor Man's Treasure

ʿAlī ibn Mahziyār al-Ahwāzī

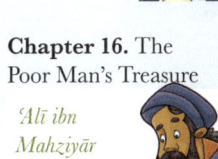

page *201*

Chapter 17. Tutor to Martyr

Ibn as-Sikkīt

page *215*

Chapter 18. One Teacher, Many Blessings

Faḍl ibn Shādhān

page *233*

Chapter 19. A Secret Birth

Aḥmad ibn Isḥāq al-Ashʿarī

page *247*

Chapter 20. The Missing Link

ʿAbdullāh ibn Jaʿfar al-Ḥimyarī

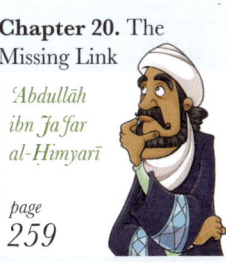

page *259*

Chapter 21. Two Promises and a Miracle

Qāsim ibn Aʿlā

page *281*

Chapter 22. Husayn's Mission

Ḥusayn ibn Rūḥ an-Nawbakhtī

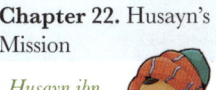

page *295*

Chapter 23. The Power of Duʿā

ʿAlī ibn Bābawayh

page *309*

Glossary

page *319*

The friends of the faithful –
How loyal they are!
They serve their Imāms
No matter how far.

Their stories inspire,
Teaching us true love,
How to be their companions,
Satisfying Allah above.

To be counted as a true friend
Of the noble household
Is worth more than
All the treasures of this world.

To be counted a friend
Of the Imām of today,
We must serve him like these heroes,
And for his return we must pray.

CHAPTER 1

In Search of Truth

Salmān al-Fārsī (Rūzbeh)

Chapter 1

Rūzbeh passes stealthily beneath the shade of green, leafy trees, clutching a hunting spear. He has one target, one aim, focused on the flicker of movement he sees ahead through the trees. A sudden crunch of leaves startles him from behind. He whirls around and comes face to face with an old man, a large book cradled in his arms.

"I hope I didn't scare you," says the man, smiling.

"I'm not afraid," Rūzbeh replies. He is silent for a moment as he gazes curiously at the book. "What are you reading?" Forever in search of truth and new knowledge, Rūzbeh's restless heart is only content when he is learning.

"I am a Christian monk, and this is the Injīl. It is the holy book revealed to Prophet ʿĪsā (ʿa) by God," explains the old man.

Rūzbeh can feel his heart pumping just a little bit faster. Maybe this is what he has been looking for! "Can you please tell me more?" he begs.

"Prophet ʿĪsā (ʿa) taught us to worship the one true God," the monk continues. "He taught us to serve others for the sake of God. He taught us to be humble, to be kind to those around us, and to share what we have with those who have less than we do. Most importantly, he taught us to always stand with truth and justice."

"Please, tell me more!" begs Rūzbeh, barely able to contain his excitement.

"Prophet ʿĪsā (ʿa) also gave us guidelines to follow in our everyday lives—rules that God has laid down for us. For example, God tells us that there are certain types of food that we should not eat, such as goat or lamb, if the meat has not been prepared properly. Because He is the one who created us, He knows what is best for us. He knows the wisdom behind these rules, even if we do not."

Rūzbeh listens with rapt attention. He recognizes a glimmer of truth in the old monk's words. What he said made sense.

"Thank you," Rūzbeh says. "I feel like I learned so much from you in just a few minutes. I would love to hear more someday."

"It was my pleasure," replies the monk. "I can see the desire for truth that burns within you. May God guide you in your journey toward that truth." He smiles and turns to leave.

"Wait!" calls Rūzbeh. "What is your name?"

"People know me as Father Abzari. God-willing, we may meet again."

Rūzbeh watches the monk disappear into the trees as the sun begins to sink below the horizon and shadows lengthen in the woods. With firm resolve, he promises himself that he will act on what he has just learned to the best of his ability. Still clutching his spear, he returns home. He knows that the deer he had been tracking earlier must be long gone by now. Now, he is hunting something else.

A few days later, the Persian king invites some visiting dignitaries to his palace for a feast. Rūzbeh accompanies his father, who is a close friend and advisor to the king.

The table is spread with fresh loaves of soft white bread and different kinds of roasted meat. Rūzbeh's mouth begins to water as tantalizing smells waft toward him. At that moment, he realizes that the meat is goat meat, and he remembers what the old Christian monk had said:

"For example, God tells us that there are certain types of food that we should not eat, such as goat or lamb, if the meat has not been prepared properly. Because He is the one who created us, He knows what is best for us. He knows the wisdom behind these rules, even if we do not."

Faithful to his promise that he would act on whatever truth he had learned from the monk, Rūzbeh takes only bread, and no meat. This does not escape the king's notice.

"Why haven't you taken any meat?" the king demands. "Do you not like my food?"

"Honorable King," Rūzbeh respectfully replies, "I learned from a Christian monk that eating the meat of a goat prepared in this way is an act disliked by God—"

"How dare you speak about such nonsense to my face!" roars the king before Rūzbeh can even finish his sentence. "How dare you try and teach me what is right and what is wrong! Who is this Christian who dares challenge my laws with the laws of his 'God'? I want him out of my kingdom at once!"

In shock, Rūzbeh backs away, deeply shaken and confused. Why did the mention of God anger the king so much? Why didn't the king want the Christian to spread his teachings? What was he trying to hide? Was he trying to hide the truth?

The very next day, by the king's decree, the wise Christian monk is forced to flee.

Meanwhile, Rūzbeh is restless. He revisits the forest, running his hand over the bark of the trees, lost in reflection. "My Lord," he prays, "I seek nearness to You, but I don't know where to start. I beg You to show me the way!"

An idea begins to form in Rūzbeh's mind. If he could find someone to teach him...

It is late at night when Rūzbeh knocks on the wooden doors of the old monastery at the edge of the city. He hears the patter of footsteps and the fiddling of a lock before the door begins to creak open.

"Who's there?" a voice whispers.

"It's Rūzbeh. I'm a friend of Father Abzari. Please, could you tell me where he has gone?"

"Why do you want to know?" the voice asks, suspicious.

"I want to ask him if he is willing to be my teacher."

There is silence for a moment as a pair of eyes gazes into Rūzbeh's face. His obvious sincerity puts an end to any doubts or suspicions. "He's gone all the way to Iraq, to the city of Mosul. But you should be able to catch up to him. Look for the Monastery of St. Elijah. God-willing, you will find him there." The door begins to close.

"Thank you," says Rūzbeh, fighting to remain calm. Then he turns and walks quickly toward his home, already planning what he will need to take with him on his journey. The road ahead of him stretches into the distance. He must soon be on his way.

The great wooden doors of the St. Elijah's Monastery make Rūzbeh feel very small. After weeks of weary travel, he is finally here, amid the bustling streets of Mosul. Once again, he raises his hand and knocks three times. This time, he cannot hear footsteps because of the noise that surrounds him. The door swings open. In the doorway stands Father Abzari, as kind and welcoming as ever.

"My dear son!" he exclaims. "What brings you all the way here?"

"Father," Rūzbeh replies, "I have come to learn. Will you teach me more about your faith?"

"It would be my pleasure; may God reward your persistence and dedication. Come." Taking him by the hand, Father Abzari leads Rūzbeh through the doorway into his new home.

For the next few months, Rūzbeh follows Father Abzari like a second shadow. In the monastery, they pray together, eat together, and read the Bible together. Father Abzari tells Rūzbeh stories of the past Prophets and lessons from the life of Prophet ʿĪsa (ʿa).

Outside on the streets, Rūzbeh helps Father Abzari serve those in need. They provide food and clothing to the poor so they can lead dignified lives. They visit the sick to provide healing and comfort. They help those who have made mistakes in the past to renew their faith and rebuild their connection to God.

"This was the example Prophet ʿĪsā (ʿa) set for his followers," Father Abzari explains. "Each day, I try to follow in his footsteps and serve the people as he served them."

The more Rūzbeh learns the teachings of Prophet ʿĪsā (ʿa), the more he is convinced that this path is the path of truth, the path that leads to God's pleasure.

One evening, before going to sleep, Rūzbeh sits on the edge of his cloak—laid out on the ground like a mattress—quiet. His eyes look to a faraway place. He raises his hands in prayer for a few moments and then sighs.

"My son, you look upset. What's bothering you?" asks Father Abzari.

Rūzbeh lifts his head to meet his mentor's gaze and replies, "Father, I wish I could've been alive at the time of Prophet ʿĪsā (ʿa) so I could serve him. It makes me sad that I will never be able to do that."

Father Abzari smiles. "My dear child, do not worry. You will still have the chance to meet and serve a great Prophet. Prophet ʿĪsā (ʿa) foretold the coming of another Prophet after him, who will also be from the family of Prophet Ibrāhīm (ʿa). He will be the last Prophet, and his name will be Aḥmad, or Muḥammad (ṣ). Through him, God will complete His message. That Prophet's message will be the final truth."

Confused, Rūzbeh asks, "Why do you say his message will be the final truth? Isn't Prophet ʿĪsā's message the final truth? Is it a different message?"

"At its core, the message is the same—the same message you were able to recognize as truth when you first heard it: belief in one God, in Prophets as guides. But there are other parts of the message that God has given us piece by piece, Prophet by Prophet, because we humans would not be ready to understand them all at once. With the last Prophet, God will have put all the pieces together to form the complete and perfect religion."

Rūzbeh's face glows with excitement. "I pray to God that I will have the honor of being his companion!"

The sun beats down on Rūzbeh's back. Sand swirls around him like snow. It has been over a day since a ferocious dust storm separated him from the caravan he was traveling with—over a day since he has seen any sign of life.

Exhausted, he stops where he is and gazes into the cloudless blue sky. His cracked lips mouth a prayer.

Years have passed since Rūzbeh left his home to live with Father Abzari. He continued to learn by Father Abzari's side until the wise monk was called back to his Lord. He had closely studied the attributes of the Prophet Muḥammad (ṣ) mentioned by Prophet ʿĪsā (ʿa) and within the original text of the Injīl—a trail of clues pointing in the Prophet's direction, toward Arabia. After years of preparation, he embarked on this journey in search of the last Prophet.

But now, he is lost. He sees something shimmer on the horizon, but by now, he knows not to trust his eyes in the simmering heat.

Then, he hears the tinkle of distant bells. He whirls around, scanning his surroundings for an approaching caravan. From behind a nearby dune, he sees a string of camels emerge.

"Thank you, my Lord!" he exclaims as he half-stumbles, half-sprints in the direction of the caravan. When he is only a few feet away, he realizes this is not the same caravan he had set out with. Before he is able to call out, two men come toward him. They grab him by the arms and steer him back toward the caravan. As the camels continue forward in keeping with the rhythm of the bells, Rūzbeh has no choice but to follow, flanked on either side by grim-faced guards.

Despite the circumstances of his rescue, Rūzbeh thanks God and follows his captors' orders without complaint. Perhaps this is a blessing in disguise.

Within a few days, Rūzbeh's new caravan reaches Medina. He is soon sold as a slave, which does not come as a surprise. After being so closely guarded during the journey, he knew what would eventually be his fate.

Life is difficult as a slave. Rūzbeh works tirelessly, day and night. During the day, he takes the sheep and searches for green pasture for them to graze. During the night, he tends to the needs of his master and his family. But even though he is no longer a free man, he is still as hopeful as ever. He has not forgotten his search for the truth or the words of Father Abzari about the great Prophet to come.

Through the pathways ordained by God, however unusual they may have been, he is here now, in Arabia. Now, he must wait and listen to his surroundings until God decides to reveal the next clues.

A wonderful fragrance fills the air as Rūzbeh prepares to take his herd of sheep to the pasture one morning. The streets are abuzz with excitement. Children scramble up the date palms at the gates of the city for a better look. Rūzbeh secures his herd and then runs to join the crowd.

"Muḥammad is coming!" he hears people whisper.

"He is here to finally make peace," someone says.

"I hear he brings a new message," says another.

"He will be the last Prophet, and his name will be Aḥmad, or Muḥammad (ṣ). Through him, God will complete his message. His message will be the final truth."

Rūzbeh's heart swells with joy. This is the moment he has worked toward for a lifetime. This is the Prophet he has longed to serve. This is the truth he has searched for since childhood.

He weaves his way through the crowd until he stands on the edge, below the dangling legs of the children in the trees. In the distance, he sees a figure on a camel approach.

Within seconds, he is overwhelmed by the force of the crowd behind him as they surge forward to greet the Prophet (ṣ). He quickly darts out of the way to avoid being trampled and takes shelter behind a date palm. His breath comes out in gasps; his heart is pounding. He leans against the date palm, breathes deeply to calm himself, and smiles. "Alḥamdulillāh," he says. In Medina, he has learned the Arabic word for God, Allah, as well as different ways to praise Him. This is one of them. He repeats the phrase to himself until the crowd begins to disperse.

His trembling legs can hardly support his weight as he makes his way to the blessed Prophet of Allah. Rūzbeh falls to his knees, but the Prophet (ṣ) immediately lifts him back up and embraces him warmly. "Salāmun ʿalaykum, Rūzbeh! I am glad to finally meet you. I know you have come a long way to see me; may Allah reward you for all your efforts to strive in His way."

"Wa ʿalaykum salām, O Messenger of Allah!" Tears stream down Rūzbeh's face as he kisses the Prophet's hand. "It brings me so much joy to see your face. I am here to learn and accept the message you bring—Allah's final and perfect message; and I am here to aid you in any way I can in spreading that message. I am your student and your servant."

Rūzbeh's search for the source of complete truth has come to an end with Prophet Muḥammad (ṣ) as his new mentor. Now, he must continue to learn that truth, practice what he learns, and defend that truth with his life if it ever comes under attack.

Epilogue

Rūzbeh goes on to become one of the Prophet's most devoted followers. He submits completely to Allah's will and the message of Islam. For this reason, the Prophet (ṣ) gives him the name "Salmān," which means "one who submits." Today, he is known by many as Salmān al-Fārsī because his roots go all the way back to Persia.

As one of the few non-Arabs in Medina, Salmān is often looked down upon by those around him. He is told by some that he does not belong here. Sometimes, he is mocked for being from a different country. But none of these cruel comments faze him.

His heart is content; he is at peace. He is by his Prophet's side—the side of all that is good and true.

And the Prophet (ṣ) comes to Salmān's aid and defends him. He teaches the people that it is wrong to treat people badly because they are from a different culture, a different tribe. In Allah's eyes, the best among all people is the one with the most taqwā—the one who is most mindful of Allah.

Because of Salmān's taqwā and sincerity, the Prophet (ṣ) bestows him with a special honor, which no other person—Arab or non-Arab—has ever received. The Prophet (ṣ) tells him, "Salmān, you are part of my Ahl al-Bayt."

As arduous as his journey has been, his reward from Allah is endless. Every step of the way, he struggled to better himself and better serve Allah. His persistence and his unwavering trust in Allah helped guide him through every trial.

Salmān's purpose in life was to meet and serve Prophet Muḥammad (ṣ), the divine leader of his time. Now, we must prepare to serve our Imām, Imām Mahdī (ʿaj), in whatever way we can. He is waiting for us.

CHAPTER 2

The Loyal Messenger

Abān ibn Abī ʿAyyāsh

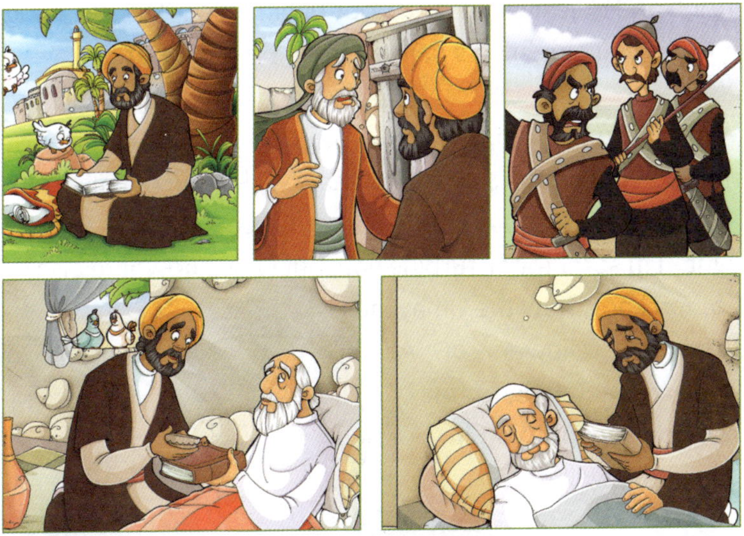

Chapter 2

It is late at night; only two hours are left until Fajr. Suddenly, there is a pounding at the door. Abān rises from his prayer mat and cautiously crosses the room. The door swings open to reveal Abān's teacher and close friend, Sulaym, clutching a leather bound book to his chest.

"Salāmun ʿalaykum!" Abān says, surprised. He ushers Sulaym inside and quickly shuts the door behind him. "What's going on? Are you alright? It's dangerous to be out so late."

"Wa ʿalaykum salām, Abān," Sulaym replies. He leans against the wall for support, breathing heavily. He is an old man, and each strand of hair in his silver beard seems to radiate a soft light. "I'm sorry for disturbing you, but I have nowhere else to go. You know how the Umayyads treat the followers of ʿAlī. They are searching for me, but now I've put you in danger as well—"

"Don't say that," Abān says, pressing Sulaym's hand reassuringly. "Please, stay. I can protect you here in my home. If the soldiers come searching for you, I will find a way to hide you, or we will face them together. We Shīʿah must stand with each other against those who want to harm us. Our shared love for ʿAlī and his children makes us closer than brothers."

Sulaym sighs and gives Abān a small, sad smile. "I don't think I can ever thank you enough."

"Besides," Abān continues earnestly, "You are like a father to me. You have taught me so much. When I first came to Basra, you and your tribe took me in like one of your own. This is only my humble way of thanking you."

For the next few weeks, Abān guards his house as though it is a fortress. There are soldiers waiting at every corner, sometimes even in disguise. They pretend to be friendly neighbors as they ask about someone who they think might be Shīʿah. These days, the governor of Basra treats being Shīʿah as the greatest crime. Like the rest of the corrupt Umayyad government, he is determined to find and punish anyone who loves and follows the Ahl al-Bayt (ʿa). Those who spread the message of the Ahl al-Bayt (ʿa)—teachers, like Sulaym—are the biggest targets.

Each day, Abān and Sulaym come up with a strategy for how to go about their business without being noticed by soldiers and spies.

"I'm not as young as I used to be, but it's hard to wait here and sit still while you go out risking your life for me every day." Sulaym tells Abān. "I wish there was something I could do to help, something even as simple as saving you a trip to the market for food!"

"Don't worry," Abān says. "We will figure out a way. Let's pray that Allah helps us figure out a way."

Over the next few days, Abān maps out his route to the market and back. He takes a long, winding way home that leads past where his sister and aunt live. This way, he is able to visit them, as well, and see if there is anything they need. It is also the perfect way to shake off anyone who might be trying to follow him.

"It's best if I go to buy our food," he tells Sulaym. "There are too many people in the market who might recognize you. Besides, you are safer here."

While Abān takes care of errands outside, Sulaym arranges to meet secretly with his students in Abān's home. His students come, one or two at a time, dressed as if they are delivering packages. Together, he and his students engage in learning and worship. When Abān returns home, he joins them as well. They share what they have learned from the Imāms (ʿa) and discuss how they can practice what they have learned, especially in such dangerous times. Each day, they pray for Allah's protection from the ruthless governor of Basra.

One day, during their discussion, they hear several people hammering angrily at the door. "Open up!" a harsh voice demands. "We have been ordered to search this house."

The two students spring to their feet, grab a large basket that is filled with dates, and pretend to be date-sellers. They bring it into the middle of the room and fill a small sack with dates as if preparing to sell them. Abān helps

Sulaym stand and guides him to a back room of his house. He lifts a rug to reveal a trapdoor built into the floor.

“Inshāʾ Allāh, you will be safe in here.” Abān promises as Sulaym opens the trapdoor and begins to carefully climb down into the secret hiding space. “It's where I keep my books to protect them from unfriendly hands.” Then, Abān quickly covers the secret door with the rug, hurries to the front door, and opens it.

“Salāmun ʿalaykum, brothers,” he says calmly to the three soldiers standing on his doorstep. He gestures for them to come inside. “Don't mind the mess; I was just finishing up some business with these date-sellers.”

The soldiers grunt in reply and walk past Abān into the house. They glance at the “date-sellers” and rummage through the large basket of dates, as if a grown man could be hiding in there. Then, they check behind the curtains hanging in front of the window. After thoroughly searching every room of the small house, they are forced to admit there is nothing there and leave without saying another word.

Abān sighs in relief and thanks Allah. He had almost forgotten to hide Sulaym's bed and belongings that morning, as he usually did, but then Allah sent a little reminder. He nods gratefully at the "date-sellers" and then goes to tell Sulaym that the danger has passed for now.

As weeks turn into months, Sulaym falls ill. Abān stays by his bedside to care for him. It is difficult to watch as the strength slowly leaves his teacher's body. It is like watching his father fade away before his eyes.

Since the time of Imām ʿAlī (ʿa), Sulaym has been a loyal follower of the Ahl al-Bayt (ʿa). Being a guardian of their knowledge has been his lifelong mission. While the Umayyads burn books out of hatred for the Ahl al-Bayt (ʿa) and ban anyone from recording ḥadīth, Sulaym has made it his job to protect books with his life so that people can continue to learn from the Imāms. When he was younger, he even maintained a secret trading network: fellow Shīʿah would borrow books from each other to copy down ḥadīth and keep the tradition of learning alive.

Now, in his old age, though his love for Imām ʿAlī (ʿa) is stronger than ever, Sulaym's body is beginning to weaken. He knows he will not remain in this world for much longer. But there is one more thing he must do before his soul leaves his body. Even during the last moments of his life, he wants to make sure he can leave something special behind for his community.

One evening, he calls out to Abān, who is kneeling by his side. His voice is very faint, but Abān notices it is filled with a new kind of strength. "Abān, you are like a son to me, and you have been very kind. I know that my death is near, but there is something very important to me that I haven't been able to do. I want to entrust this task to you." Sulaym looks into Abān's eyes, searching for a response.

Abān takes Sulaym's hand and gently kisses it. "Tell me what I need to do, and with Allah's help I will do it."

Encouraged, Sulaym continues. "These past few years, I have been compiling a book of ḥadīth. There is so much I have learned from my master ʿAlī, and I want others to be able to learn from his teachings as well." Sulaym struggles to sit up. He reaches for his cloak, folded beside him, and begins to unfold it. Hidden inside is the leather-bound book he had brought with him that first night. "I want to entrust it to you," he says again, offering Abān the book. "Make sure that it reaches the children of ʿAlī safely. It must never be lost or destroyed."

Abān carefully takes the book from Sulaym and holds it close to his chest. "I will guard it with my life," he promises. "I can only imagine how hard you must have worked to preserve this knowledge. It is truly a treasure."

Abān looks at Sulaym for a long moment and gently strokes his papery wrinkled hand. Sulaym's eyes are closed, but his lips slowly mouth the shahādah:

"I testify that there is no god but Allah, and that Muḥammad is His Messenger." Then, his lips stop moving, and the old man lies still.

After burying Sulaym with his own hands, Abān gazes at the book, wiping tears from his eyes. Although it is light, it feels heavy in his hands because of how precious it is, and because of how much Sulaym sacrificed for its sake. Remembering the circumstances under which the book has come to him, Abān feels the weight of this trust. The Umayyads have destroyed so many treasure troves of knowledge out of their hatred for everything good—including students, scholars, and even entire libraries. Only a handful of books have survived.

He begins to flip through the book and is awed by the beauty and wisdom of the words on each page. Truly, it is a priceless treasure.

Finally, he closes the book. He knows he must take it to the family of the Prophet (ṣ) without delay. The month of Dhul Ḥijjah is drawing near, and people from all over the Muslim lands will flock to Mecca for Ḥajj. He knows that is one place where the Shīʿah will be able to come together without facing outright persecution. He knows that is one place where he will be able to find the Imām (ʿa). Above all, he knows that Allah is the Lord of the Kaʿbah, and that if he seeks refuge in Allah and His House, he may finally be able to find some peace after the hardships he has faced in the past months. He prays to Allah that he will be able to enjoy the blessings of this sacred pilgrimage, fulfill his promise to Sulaym, and find comfort in meeting his beloved Imām Sajjād (ʿa). He decides it is best to make preparations for his journey at once. The road from Basra to Mecca is a long one, especially when traveling by foot.

Abān arrives in Mecca sometime before the rituals of Ḥajj officially begin. The Kaʿbah looms into view as he enters Masjid al-Ḥarām. Many worshippers have already gathered to pray or recite Qurʾān in the blessed shadow of the Kaʿbah. As he comes closer, he sees that one group is loosely clustered around Maqām Ibrāhīm, the stone that Prophet

Ibrāhīm (ʿa) used as a stepping stool when rebuilding the Kaʿbah, which has his footprints miraculously embedded in it forever. Standing on the tips of his toes, Abān peers into the center of the cluster and notices a man in sajdah. Even from a distance, Abān can sense the intensity of the man's conversation with Allah. In this moment, the world around him no longer matters. Abān stands, mesmerized, watching who he knows to be the Imām (ʿa).

Abān feels himself trembling uncontrollably. His heart urges him to rush to the Imām's side at once. After the turmoil and grief of the past months, he longs to embrace the Imām (ʿa) and let all his worries slip off his shoulders. But, at the same time, he is hesitant, and butterflies flutter in his stomach. To be so close to the Imām (ʿa) fills him with awe. Unsure of how to proceed, Abān walks toward the cluster, sits off to the side, and begins to recite Qurʾān to calm his nerves. Even though Arabic is not his first language, his beautiful recitation outmatches that of most Arabs. As he recites under his breath, a wonderful melody fills his mind, and he loses himself in the meaning of the verses.

"Salāmun ʿalaykum, Abān," says a voice beside him. Abān looks up and sees the Imām (ʿa) smiling at him. "Your recitation is beautiful, even when it is barely louder than a whisper. It reflects the beauty of your soul."

Abān scrambles to his feet to kiss the Imām's hand. "Wa ʿalaykum salām, my Imām. I can only try to bring the beauty of Allah's words to life."

The Imām (ʿa) looks into Abān's eyes. "You seem tired," he observes. "You've come a long way. Either you carry a very great treasure or a very heavy burden, or both."

Abān gives a small half-smile. "Both," he says. Abān brings out the book from his bag and holds it out for the Imām (ʿa) to take. "Here is the treasure. It is a gift—an offering—from Sulaym ibn al-Qays. It is his compilation of ḥadīth he has learned from your fathers. His dying wish was that you should have it, so it will be safe from your enemies." He pauses as Sulaym's death flashes before his eyes.

"May Allah grant him a special place in Paradise," says the Imām (ʿa) in a low voice as he takes the book. "It saddens me to hear that he has passed away. Thank you, Abān. You have been a loyal messenger."

The two embrace and share a moment of silent mourning before Abān continues, spilling out everything he has kept bottled up for so long. "But the burden—it's just that we've had to hide for so long. We've had to live in fear, afraid that every move we make is being watched by those who want to hurt us. How much longer will we have to hide?"

"This is a difficult time for our Shīʿah," replies the Imām (ʿa). "It is Allah's way of testing our devotion and strengthening our trust and faith in Him. But it will not always be like this. Inshāʾallāh, there will come a day when we no longer have to hide. Abān, you will live to see better times when my son, Muḥammad, and my grandson, Jaʿfar, will be able to teach much more freely than I. Continue to cherish the love you have for us, and Allah will continue to reward you for it and guide you on your way."

Abān nods. He feels the burden he has carried with himself for so long slip off his shoulders. Here, in the shadow of Allah's House, where Islam first took root, at Imām Sajjād's side, Abān is able to find peace at last.

CHAPTER 3

The Thirsty Water Bearer

Abū Yazīd Ṭayfūr al-Basṭāmī (as-Saqqā')

Chapter 3

It looks like stars are fluttering to earth. Snowflakes spin in small swirls at the edge of the road as Ṭayfūr returns home for the night. The fading light and gathering dark signal that it is prayer time. He tucks his book under his cloak and hugs himself against the slight chill. Within a few minutes, he comes to his home and knocks gently on the door. A smiling woman opens it wide.

"Salāmun ʿalaykum, Ṭayfūr! You're home! Come in quickly; you must be so cold."

"Wa ʿalaykum salām, dearest mother." Ṭayfūr hugs her tightly as the dusting of snow on his cloak melts and disappears.

"I'm glad you're home," his mother says before they let go. Before walking to the other end of the room to prepare for wuḍūʾ, she asks, "Ṭayfūr—would you bring me the jug of water by the door?"

"Of course," Ṭayfūr replies. "You know I'd do anything for you." He glances at the water jug; it's empty. "Just one moment."

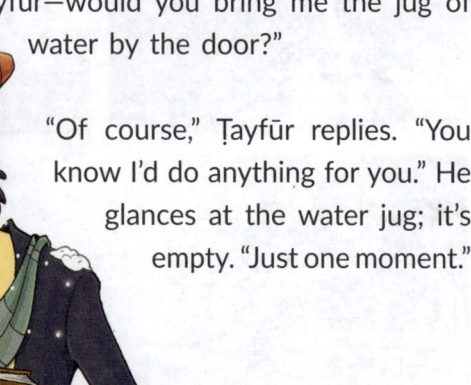

He quickly wraps himself in his cloak again, grabs the jug, slips out the door, and heads toward the well nearby. Before he casts the bucket into the well, he places his hands on the stone ledge that surrounds it and gazes into its depths for a long moment. In the presence of so much water, Ṭayfūr is reminded of his intense thirst—not for water, but for knowledge.

Since he was very young, Ṭayfūr has always intensely craved knowledge, learning, and wisdom, and he has spent his life in search of something to satisfy this need. Despite studying in over 30 different cities, under 113 different scholars, he is not yet satisfied. He has not yet reached the source.

The thirst for knowledge still raging silently within him, Ṭayfūr throws the bucket into the well, fills the water jug, and returns to the house. The jug is cold in his hands, but he doesn't mind. He's doing it for his mother. He knows that Jannah lies under her feet, and that serving her is the key to his success.

When he reenters his house, his mother has just finished laying out the prayer rugs.

"I've brought you some water," Ṭayfūr says, holding out the water jug.

"Thank you, my son. May Allah bless you."

She turns around to take the jug from him and gasps as her hands brush his. "Oh! Your hands are frozen!"

Ṭayfūr smiles and gives his mother's hand a comforting squeeze. "Don't worry—they'll warm up in a little while." He gestures at the water jug. "Bismillāh. Please, go ahead."

Long after Ṭayfūr finishes praying Maghrib and ʿIshāʾ, his mother remains on her prayer rug, her hands raised in prayer. He lies in bed and watches her tenderly.

Every now and then, he hears her murmur Allah's name or send ṣalawāt on the Prophet (ṣ) and his family. She has always been a role model for him. She raised him to be a good Muslim, dedicated to serving Allah, and she has never once stopped praying for him. Ṭayfūr knows the value of a mother's duʿā, and he strives to make himself worthy of these duʿās. Even though he knows he can never repay her for all that she has done for him, he hopes and prays that he can continue to show his love for her by bringing her happiness in whatever way he can.

His mind takes him back to the well, the water, and his burning desire to quench his thirst for knowledge from the source. Soon, his mother's soothing voice as she recites dhikr and duʿā lulls him to sleep.

As the months pass, winter's chill melts into spring. The beautiful gardens that line the streets lift Ṭayfūr's spirits. He meets with his students under the shade of the palms and mingles with his fellow Muslims in the marketplace.

"Salāmun ʿalaykum, Abu Yazīd!" he hears someone call out from behind him, respectfully addressing him by his kunyah.

Ṭayfūr turns around and smiles. It is his student, Ḥāmid, who always has a question on the tip of his tongue. "Wa ʿalaykum salām, Ḥāmid. What can I do for you?"

"Abu Yazīd, you've taught me so much, but I don't know what I'm going to do when I don't have you as my teacher anymore—if I move to another city, if we are no longer able to meet. Please, can you tell me where I must turn in order to find true knowledge?"

Ṭayfūr pauses for a moment before answering. He sees his younger self reflected in Ḥāmid's expectant face. How many times has he asked his teachers that same question? And how many more times has he asked it of himself? He offers Ḥāmid the same answer his teachers would tell him.

"You must take it from the source."

Ḥāmid beams with gratitude, but he is not yet satisfied. Shyly, he asks, "Can you please tell me more?"

Again, Ṭayfūr pauses. He studies Ḥāmid's face, and then replies, weighing his words carefully. "Beware of arrogance. If you seek knowledge to satisfy your pride, then every step will take you further from the truth."

Ḥāmid nods and promises to heed the warning. "Thank you," he says. "Inshāʾ Allāh I will be able to practice what you've taught me today." He says his salāms and continues on his way.

As Ṭayfūr walks home later that afternoon, he reflects on the advice he gave Ḥāmid: You take it from the source.

It is a short answer—almost like a riddle—but it has led Ṭayfūr in the right direction. He hopes Ḥāmid will be able to benefit from it as well. His teachers have taught him to turn to the Qurʾān and the Prophet's family for guidance. They are the links to the ultimate source: Allah.

At the same time, they have always warned against arrogance. Knowledge is light, they would say, but only those with pure hearts can access it. Arrogance and pride block the way to understanding. They lead toward selfishness and turn you away from Allah and the truth. They form a barrier, which the light of knowledge cannot shine through.

Ṭayfūr's mind drifts to thoughts of Imām Ṣādiq (ʿa) in Medina. Again, the same phrase floats to the surface of his mind. Take it from the source. That is the advice he gave to Ḥāmid, but what about himself? Just because he is a teacher doesn't mean he is done learning. He still shares every bit of Ḥāmid's eagerness to learn. Isn't it time to take the steps to quench that thirst? Isn't it time to continue this lifelong quest for truth? He decides that it is. It is time to pay his Imām (ʿa) a visit.

Soon after his conversation with Ḥāmid, Ṭayfūr confides in his mother his wish to travel to Medina and become a student of Imām Ṣādiq (ʿa). "But I don't want to leave you!" he says to her with tears in his eyes. "I wish you could come with me, but the journey is long and hard. Please, tell me whatever you think is best, and I will do it."

Ṭayfūr's mother hesitates for a moment. "Medina is so far away," she says. "We wouldn't really be able to visit each other. And you might end up being gone for a long time… "

Ṭayfūr gently takes his mother's hand and kisses it. "If you want me to stay, I will happily stay with you. I want to be here for you just like you've always been here for me."

"I still want you to go and learn," she says finally, completing her thought. "I really do. It brings me joy to see your devotion to Allah and your Imām and your desire to learn. You need to go to Medina so you can continue to learn and grow. I will pray for your safety and success every day. I will miss you very much, though; don't forget to write to me. And convey my salāms to the Imām (ʿa). I wish I could meet him in person as well."

"InshāʾAllah, I will write to you, and I will also come and visit as much as I can," Ṭayfūr promises. He feels much better knowing that he has his mother's blessings. "It would be impossible to forget you. You will always be in my heart."

"Alḥamdulillāh!" Ṭayfūr shouts as the silhouettes of Medina's palm trees appear on the horizon. It is as if they are inviting him to come and enjoy their cool shade. It has been a long journey—over a thousand miles—but with Allah's blessing and his mother's duʿā, Ṭayfūr safely enters the streets of Medina.

His throat is parched, and his lips are cracked. It has been almost a day since he finished whatever water he was carrying with him. But he hardly notices the heat and how thirsty he is because of a thirst that is much greater—a thirst for knowledge. A wonderful smell fills the air around him, like the fragrance of a special flower. Before doing anything else, he visits the Prophet's Mosque and the graves of the Imāms who are buried in Jannat al-Baqīʾ. The visit refreshes him, reminds him of his goals, and encourages him to continue forward.

Soon afterward, Ṭayfūr spots a group of young men engaged in a serious discussion. Some of them have books open in their lap and are taking notes. He can tell they are students; perhaps they can lead him to their teacher.

"Salāmun ʿalaykum, brothers," he greets them. "I couldn't help but overhear your conversation. I'm also a student, and I would love to learn more from you. May I ask who is your teacher?"

“He is our Imām, Jaʿfar aṣ-Ṣādiq,” one man replies.

Ṭayfūr’s heart leaps. “Can you tell me where I can meet him?” he asks.

“Yes,” the same man replies as he gets to his feet. “If you follow me, I can show you where he lives.”

A few minutes later, Ṭayfūr stands on the doorstep of Imām Ṣādiq (ʿa). His heart thumps wildly in his chest. He raises a trembling fist and knocks on the door. He hears footsteps from inside, and the door opens.

"Salāmun ʿalaykum," says the Imām (ʿa) with a warm smile. "You've come a long way, and you must be thirsty. Please, come in!" Although Ṭayfūr's face glows with excitement, the Imām (ʿa) can see that he is weary from his travels.

"Wa ʿalaykum salām, O grandson of the Messenger of Allah! My mother sends you her salāms as well." Ṭayfūr kisses the Imām's hand and steps into the house. He can hardly contain his excitement. The thrill of being with the Imām courses through his body, but at the same time, he is so overwhelmed that he can hardly speak.

Inside, the Imām (ʿa) offers Ṭayfūr water and asks him why he has come.

"I am here to learn," Ṭayfūr replies, "and I know that you are the gateway to Allah's knowledge. I've come to ask if you will accept me as your student—and if you will grant me the honor of serving your household."

"I can see that you are thirsty," says the Imām (ʿa), smiling slightly, "but not for water. This thirst of yours is a blessing. It would be my pleasure to have you as my student."

Inspired by the bowl of water he holds in his hands, Ṭayfūr looks up and says, "And it would be my pleasure to be your water bearer." He remembers drawing water from the well for his mother so many months before, and decides that he wants to help and serve the Imām (ʿa) the same way he has always served his mother.

Ṭayfūr spends 13 happy years in Medina. He treasures the precious time he spends with the Imām (ʿa) learning new and wonderful things, and he wholeheartedly enjoys being the Imām's water bearer. Each morning, he draws water from the well to do wuḍūʾ. He splashes the cool, pure water on his face and lets it trickle down his beard. Then, he fills all the jugs, waters the plants and flowers, tends to the camels and horses, and finally makes sure there is plenty of water in the house for the Imām (ʿa) and his family to use.

One day, the Imām (ʿa) stands quietly in the corner of the courtyard, watching Ṭayfūr perform his morning routine—how he lovingly cups the clear water in his hands when doing wuḍūʾ; how he cradles each water jug in his arms; how he stops every now and then to admire a blossoming flower; how he strokes the horses' glossy coats and runs his fingers through their mane. Truly, he carries out his task of providing water with tender, loving care and finds pleasure in serving Allah and his Imām (ʿa).

Once he is finished, the Imām (ʿa) calls out to Ṭayfūr and walks with him for a while. Then, he begins to speak. "My dear Ṭayfūr, I know you are very happy here, learning. But I think you will also find great happiness in sharing what you have learned with others, just like you find such happiness in providing water to the plants and animals in this courtyard. It's time for you to return home and share the gems of wisdom you now have with the people of your city. With learning comes the responsibility to help others learn as well."

Ṭayfūr's eyes fill with tears. It saddens him to leave the Imām's side, but he is honored that the Imām (ʿa) has entrusted him with such a task. "Yes, my master," he replies. "If you think that's best, then I'm content. My heart is still thirsty for your knowledge, but I am happy to help quench the thirst of those in my own city."

The Imām (ʿa) embraces his loyal student to reassure him and strengthen his resolve. "I will send two of my sons with you to keep you company on your way home," he promises. "May Allah make the path that lies ahead easy for you."

Ṭayfūr gazes at his beloved Imām (ʿa) one last time, and then begins to prepare for the journey home.

"Thank you for being my teachers and friends," Ṭayfūr says when he and his companions arrive at the city limits. "I pray that we meet again." Even after they bid each other farewell, Ṭayfūr watches them until they disappear into the distance.

Soon, whatever sadness he feels at having left Medina fades away. Being back home brings back so many good memories, and he quickens his pace as he approaches home. He hasn't seen his mother in years. He thanks Allah that she is still alive and well; they wrote letters back and forth, and he even traveled back to visit her a few times, but he misses her gentle smile and whispered prayers.

An exciting and important task lies before him. The Imām (ʿa) gave him newfound purpose as a teacher, and he is eager to be among his students again. In a way, he is still a water bearer, striving to quench the thirst of those in pursuit of knowledge and nearness to Allah.

CHAPTER 4

The Careful Student

Ḥurayth ibn ʿAbdullāh

The sound of the wind picks up outside. A slight breeze finds its way through an open window and rustles the papers on the desk. Ḥurayth closes his eyes and enjoys a breath of fresh autumn air before picking up his pen and continuing to write.

Ḥurayth ibn ʿAbdullāh is a great scholar and teacher in the city of Sīstān, famous for recording and compiling ḥadīth. He sleeps just enough to refresh himself each night and devotes the rest of his time to writing, teaching, and worshipping Allah.

There is a knock on the door. Ḥurayth smiles. He can already guess who it might be. While many students come to study with him, none of them is as dedicated and persistent as Ḥammād.

Ḥurayth opens the door wide and welcomes Ḥammād inside. "Salāmun ʿalaykum, Ḥammād! It is good to see you. Have you come for another book?"

Ḥammād grins and holds out a leather-bound book. "Wa ʿalaykum salām. Yes, please. I've just finished another round of studying your book on the rules of ṣalāh. There is so much to learn from these pages. I don't think I'll ever get tired of reviewing it over and over again. I discover something new every time!"

"I'm glad you find it helpful," Ḥurayth says, trying to hide his smile. "You are truly tireless when it comes to learning."

"I've learned that from you," Ḥammād replies. The two share a special bond that goes beyond that of student and teacher. It is more like the bond of a father and son.

"Come and sit down," Ḥurayth says, gesturing to a cushioned seat on the floor. He sets a bowl of fruit down in front of Ḥammād, and then joins him on the floor. "And have some fruit."

"Only if you'll eat with me," Ḥammād says, offering an apple to his teacher.

"I'll eat later. Don't wait for me," Ḥurayth says. "You enjoy it."

At this point, Ḥammād realizes that Ḥurayth must be fasting. He pauses for a moment, apple in hand, unsure of what to do. He is reluctant to eat while his teacher is fasting, but he doesn't want to reject what his teacher has so kindly offered either. Then he smiles and lets the apple rest in his lap. He will take it with him and eat it later.

Always eager to learn, Ḥammād asks, "Will you please tell me a ḥadīth from one of our Imāms? I feel like I need a reminder."

"Perhaps this will help: Imām Bāqir (ʿa) has said that if someone fasts all day and prays all night, performs Ḥajj, and gives away all his wealth as charity, his actions are worth nothing if he does not obey and follow the Imāms."

Ḥammād nods, his brow furrowed in concentration as he tries to connect this to what he has learned before. "Because we must obey the Imāms if we truly want to please Allah," he says as he thinks out loud. "They are His representatives and guides, so we must follow them. In order to earn Allah's pleasure, we must earn theirs. That's the path we need to take toward true success."

Ḥurayth gazes at Ḥammād with fatherly pride in his eyes. "May Allah continue to grant you the motivation to learn and memorize ḥadīth."

"Again, it's what I've learned from you," Ḥammād says humbly. "I probably should be heading home now. Thank you for the reminder and the fruit." As he gets to his feet and helps his teacher to rise, he grins shyly and asks, "May I take your book on ṣalāh home one more time? I still feel like my notes are incomplete."

Ḥurayth pats Ḥammād on the back and chuckles. "You are always welcome to take my books."

As Ḥammād returns home, he cups his apple in both hands and takes a small bite. The autumn breeze rustles past his cloak, and the aroma of the apple fills the air.

Ḥurayth watches fondly from the window and thanks Allah that he has been blessed with such a considerate and sincere student.

As winter settles over Sīstān like a blanket, the chill never dampens Ḥammād's spirits. Yet he is quiet, always deep in thought and reflection. The advice from Imām Bāqir (ʿa) that his teacher shared has been weighing on his mind: "If someone fasts all day and prays all night, performs Ḥajj, and gives away all his wealth as charity, his actions are worth nothing if he does not obey and follow the Imāms." Ḥammād has always followed the example of the Imāms. He has always given greatest importance to their guidelines and commands. However, he still feels that a great distance separates him from his masters. There is an emptiness in his life he longs to fill.

One frigid morning, he makes his way to his teacher's home with an extra spring in his step.

"I've been thinking about the ḥadīth you shared with me some months ago," Ḥammād says as he joins his teacher for a cup of early morning tea, "about the importance of following our Imāms. I think I need to reconnect with the Imām of my time, our master, Imām Ṣādiq (ʿa). I've decided to go and meet him."

Ḥurayth smiles. "You speak so calmly, but I can see the joy radiating from your face. I am very happy for you." Ḥurayth is silent for a moment as memories of his times in Medina flood his mind. Especially in his younger days, he had traveled often to Medina and returned each time with newfound treasures from the stores of the Imām's wisdom. With age, the journey became more difficult. Now, it has been years since his last visit.

Ḥammād notices the wistful look in his teacher's eyes. "I will be sure to convey your salāms to the Imām," he assures Ḥurayth. "It is the least I can do after all you have done for me."

"Allāhu Akbar, Allāhu Akbar!" As Ḥammād's caravan enters Medina, the adhān penetrates the air, summoning everyone to prayer. The entire city stops its activities and heads toward the Prophet's Mosque. Sighs of relief sweep through the weary caravan as some people raise their hands in duʿā out of gratitude to Allah.

While the others gather their belongings and prepare to rest, Ḥammād does wuḍūʾ and joins the wave of people on their way to the masjid. Everything else can wait. First, he must see the Imām (ʿa).

After prayer, Ḥammād waits in the shadow of a pillar until most of the crowd filters out of the masjid. He sees Imām Ṣādiq (ʿa) near the miḥrāb, shaking hands with a last group of men. On his way out, the Imām (ʿa) glances in the direction of Ḥammād's pillar, pauses, and begins walking toward it. Ḥammād's pulse quickens as the Imām (ʿa) approaches him.

"Salāmun ʿalaykum," says the Imām (ʿa) kindly. "You must be a traveler; I don't remember seeing you before. What is your name?"

"Wa ʿalaykum salām, my Imām," Ḥammād says, swallowing hard, "I am a student of your student, Ḥurayth ibn ʿAbdullāh. My name is Ḥammād."

"It is good to see you, Ḥammād," the Imām (ʿa) says with a warm smile. "How is my old friend?"

"Alḥamdulillāh, he is well," replies Ḥammād. "He is still dedicated to compiling your teachings. He wishes very much that he could be here and sends you his salāms."

The Imām (ʿa) nods. "Please convey my salāms to him and tell him that I miss him very much as well. I remember the last time he was here, he was working on a book on ṣalāh. Are you familiar with it?"

Ḥammād's eyes light up. "Oh, yes. I have read it many times, and each time I read it, I learn something new that I didn't pick up before. Every time, it has something new to offer. I can never say that I am done with it."

"Then you probably know the rules and guidelines for ṣalāh very well," says the Imām (ʿa).

Ḥammād humbly shakes his head. "I still have a long way to go. What I know is nothing compared to what you know. I have come here to learn from you, follow you, and try my best to be like you."

The Imām (ʿa) gently places his hand on Ḥammād's shoulder. "You are a careful student, Ḥammād; and Ḥurayth is a worthy teacher. Rest now, and come to my home tomorrow. Then, I will try to help you in your quest in whatever way I can."

"Thank you, my master," Ḥammād says gratefully before bidding farewell to the Imām (ʿa). Once he steps outside the masjid, a familiar fragrance wafts toward him—the sweetness of an apple. It reminds him of home, his teacher, and a certain special book. It also reminds him that his teacher's heart is here, with him, in Medina, eager to learn something new.

Epilogue

That night, Ḥammād spends some extra time on his prayer rug. He has changed out of his traveler's clothes into a clean, white robe. A fragrant perfume fills the air as he raises his hands in duʿā and bends for rukūʿ and sajdah. His gaze is focused directly in front of him to help prevent his mind from wandering.

Prayer has always been a way for him to build a special connection with Allah. This connection is a source of strength and inspiration for him, every single day. The more he prays, the stronger this connection becomes. In hard times, he turns to Allah for comfort and support. In good times, he thanks Allah for his blessings and bounties.

He thanks Allah again for bringing him safely to his Imām (ʿa) in Medina and prays that what he learns tomorrow will give him strength, increase him in faith, and help make his prayer more like his Imām's prayer.

As always, he makes sure to pray for his teacher, Ḥurayth, who has helped him come this far in his journey to get closer to Allah.

CHAPTER 5

The Young Sage

Jābir ibn Ḥayyān

Since childhood, his father's pharmacy has been a very special place for Jābir. As a young boy, he followed his father around the shop like a second shadow, watching closely as ingredients were gathered, prepared, and then mixed into medicines. But his favorite part wasn't making medicine; it was giving the medicine to those who needed it. Now that he is older, he has begun to take an interest in his father's books as well. He is delighted to find books filled with the wisdom of the Imāms regarding all aspects of Allah's creation, including both the spiritual and physical realms. From his father's library, he learns about Islamic beliefs, practices, and ethics, as well as chemistry, medicine, and other scientific fields.

From all this training early in his youth, Jābir grows to become a learned young man, and the people of Ṭūs call him "the Young Sage" and "the Pride of Ṭūs."

One day, Jābir helps his mother prepare a fresh batch of ingredients while his father is away. Just as they are tidying up their work space, Jābir's father, Ḥayyān, bursts through the door. He is out of breath, and his face is flushed, shining with excitement.

"We must prepare to leave Ṭūs," he says once he catches his breath.

"Why?" asks Jābir's mother, surprised.

"Remember—we talked about this." Ḥayyān replies, "It's so we can be closer to our master, Imām Ṣādiq (ʿa). I thought we both decided it was for the best."

"I know, but why now?" Jābir's mother asks, "and how?"

"There is a group of Shīʿah preparing to leave for Medina tomorrow. It's the perfect opportunity, and I don't know if we'll ever get another like it."

Jābir's mother relaxes and nods her head. "Alḥamdulillāh. Allah has answered our prayers!" Jābir is silent, but his heart leaps for joy. He just has one question.

"Father, what will we do with our pharmacy? Who will take care of our patients once we're gone?"

Ḥayyān replies, "I sold the pharmacy last week. Inshāʾ Allāh it is in good hands. We'll plan to open a new pharmacy in Medina near our Imām."

Jābir smiles to himself. His mother is right; their prayers really are being answered, almost all at once. His dearest dream is becoming true. Until now, he has only known the Imām (ʿa) through whatever words he has read in books.
Now, he has the chance to know the Imām (ʿa) through the words that come straight from his lips.

In his room, Jābir gazes fondly at the books that line his bookshelves. He tries to calculate how many camels it would take to transport them all from Ṭūs to Medina, but then chuckles and shakes his head. He will have to think of another solution.

He selects a book from the shelf and thumbs through the pages. Like many of the books in the room, it is a book he himself has written, a compilation of what he has learned from his father. Like most books at the time, it is the only existing copy. Each book must be written by hand, and the only way to create another copy is to write out the entire text, by hand, all over again. Because of this, every book in Jābir's library is a unique, priceless treasure.

But as Jābir looks at his work, he feels that it is missing something: a connection to the ultimate source of knowledge. His face brightens as he thinks of the new life that lies ahead for him and his family, in the Imām's own neighborhood in Medina. "O Allah, increase me in knowledge!"[1] he silently prays.

Setting the book back on the shelf, he grabs his prayer mat and lays it on the floor, seeking strength and inspiration in a conversation with Allah. After offering a two rakʿah prayer, he raises his hands in duʿā and begs Allah with all his heart: "Help me become a student of my Imām!"

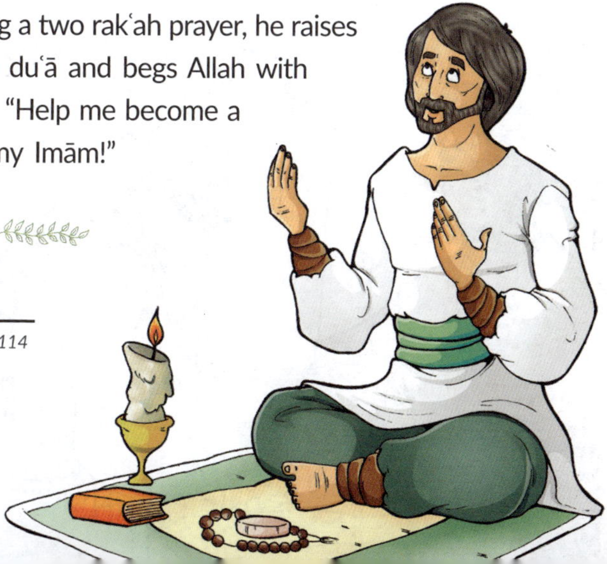

1 Noble Qurʿān, 20:114

The following morning, Jābir's home is abuzz with last-minute packing. Jābir is in his room with his good friend ʿAmmār by his side. A few books are carefully wrapped and tucked under Jābir's arm, but the rest are still arranged on his shelf. During the night, he'd had an idea. He'd remembered ʿAmmār, who had always shown great interest in learning about whatever he could, and he'd decided ʿAmmār was the perfect person to gift all these books to. Besides, the pharmacy was now under the care of ʿAmmār's father. The bond of trust between the two families was strong.

"I hope they serve you well," Jābir says, placing his hand on ʿAmmār's shoulder. "I hope they fuel your passion for learning."

"Thank you," ʿAmmār replies. "I'm honored that you've entrusted me with such a treasure."

"It's not a trust. It's a gift. These are for you," Jābir says seriously.

"Then I will treasure this gift for life," ʿAmmār says. "My father will continue your father's work as a pharmacist, and I will continue your work as a student."

Outside, as Jābir helps his parents load the last items on their camel, ʿAmmār asks, "Jābir, since you're going to see our Imām, will you convey to him my salāms?" Though he is smiling, tears sparkle in his eyes.

"Of course!" Jābir promises his friend. "I won't forget you while I am gone."

"Jābir, you are the pride of Ṭūs. I can only imagine what you will grow to be in Medina! I am very happy for you."

Humbly, Jābir says, "Thank you; I pray that Allah keeps you safe and opens many doors for you. Please keep me in your prayers as well."

They embrace like brothers one last time as a final farewell.

The 1900-mile journey is hot and dangerous, but Jābir's family cheerfully face the everyday struggles of such a long trek. After months and months of traveling, Jābir's family finally reaches Medina.

The first thing Jābir and his father do when they arrive at the city is visit Imām Ṣādiq ('a). These visits become part of their day-to-day life. Jābir's mind is always brimming with questions. His curiosity leads him from questions about science and medicine to questions about Allah, Allah's creation, and his connection to Allah. He quickly becomes one of the Imām's brightest students.

As the years pass, Jābir's accomplishments increase. He writes countless books, numbering in the thousands. His entire house is transformed into a library. Every step of the way, the Imām ('a) is there to guide and encourage him. He becomes well-known throughout the Muslim world for spreading knowledge and wisdom far and wide.

Despite all this, Jābir never forgets the source of his success. Deep inside, he knows how indebted he is to his teachers, especially to the Imām (ʿa). And he knows that he owes everything to Allah. He includes something to remind him of this in every book he writes:

"My master Imām Ṣādiq (ʿa) said to me..."

"All of my knowledge is from the knowledge of my master, Imām Ṣādiq (ʿa)."

"By Allah's grace, I have learned..."

Epilogue

As a student, Jābir knows the value of his teachers. As a Muslim, Jābir knows his place before Allah. He remains mindful of the fact that all his achievements are by the grace of his Lord.

He is remembered not only by Shīʿah as a student of Imām Ṣādiq (ʿa), but also for the contributions he made in chemistry, physics, astronomy, mathematics, medicine, and other fields. To this day, some of his books are in the great libraries of Europe.

Jābir's journey as a student, scientist, and scholar reminds us that the spiritual world and the physical world are connected, not separate. Both are part of Allah's creation and are governed by His laws. Studying physical sciences can lead to an even greater appreciation of what Allah has created and helps us better understand the world around us. This, in turn, can help strengthen our faith and inspire us to better worship and serve our Creator.

CHAPTER 6

Comfort, Shelter, and Shade

ʿImrān ibn ʿAbdullāh

Pilgrims from across the Muslim world flood Mecca. The Kaʿbah—the house of Allah—is like a magnet that draws them all close. Among the thousands in the crowd is ʿImrān ibn ʿAbdullāh. For weeks, he has prepared eagerly for his journey, and while his travel bag is heavier than most, he wears it with pride. Inside the bag is a gift—a gift for Imām Ṣādiq (ʿa).

ʿImrān scans the crowd for a glimpse of his Imām (ʿa), but it is difficult to see past all the people around him. He focuses on keeping his footing, and prays that his chance will come during the next few blessed days.

As the crowd pushes him along to where he needs to go, ʿImrān's memory wanders to a different journey: the journey from his hometown, Qom, to the Imām's home in Medina. It is a path he has travelled many times in the past, but, in recent years, he hasn't been able to make the journey. The distance between Qom and Medina has separated ʿImrān from his Imām (ʿa) for too long, and he desperately hopes that this Ḥajj will bring them together again.

It is the day of ʿArafah. From Ẓuhr to Maghrib, on the plains of ʿArafāt, ʿImrān spends his time in worship. His hands are raised in sincere duʿā. As his lips form the words of Imām Ḥusayn's duʿā, tears stream down his face.

"How shall I complain to You of my condition, when You already know my complaint? How shall I ask you for my needs, when You already know what they are? Will You disappoint my hope, while I have faith in You?"[1]

He is certain that the Imām (ʿa) is somewhere nearby, deep in prayer, a part of the flock of worshippers in white scattered across the plain. He yearns to meet him more than ever.

1 Duʿā of Imām Ḥusayn (ʿa) on the Day of ʿArafah

During the next few days, ʿImrān performs the duties of Ḥajj with renewed hope:

At Muzdalifah, he stoops to collect pebbles for the stoning of the Jamarāt, along with thousands of other scrabbling hands. As he does so, he calls to mind his mistakes and resolves never to repeat them. Just as Prophet Ibrāhīm (ʿa) and his family stoned Shayṭān when he tried to convince them to defy Allah's orders, ʿImrān prays that he can also free himself of Shayṭān's whisperings by stoning the Jamarāt. He hopes that this act will rekindle his relationship with Allah and bring him closer to his Lord.

At Mina, he stands his ground amid the throng, clutching the pebbles he has collected, focusing his aim on the pillar that looms before him. One. Two. Three. Four. Five. Six. Seven. Each stone hits its mark. Today, he must only stone the first of the Jamarāt, Jamarat al-ʿAqabah. Then, he selects a sheep from a herd of thousands and sacrifices it for Allah's pleasure, as Prophet Ibrāhīm (ʿa) had done thousands of years before. After that, he shaves his head in keeping with Allah's command. In Mecca, he performs ṭawāf and saʿy, following in the footsteps of Lady Hājar (ʿa).

Still, the Imām (ʿa) is nowhere to be seen.

That night, on the 11th of Dhul Ḥijjah, ʿImrān returns to Mina to camp for the evening. He pitches his tent alongside his fellow pilgrims. A bundle of cloth peeks out of his bag—something special that he has sewn with his own two hands.

There is a sudden commotion in the distance as four men struggle against a collapsing white tent. ʿImrān rushes to their aid and grabs a tent post to hold it steady. Together, they work to raise the tent and anchor it to the ground so it doesn't fall over again. As ʿImrān returns to his tent, he notices a group of pilgrims gathered in a circle. A hush falls over the crowd, and he can hear a familiar voice floating through the evening air. He closes his eyes as the voice leads him down memory

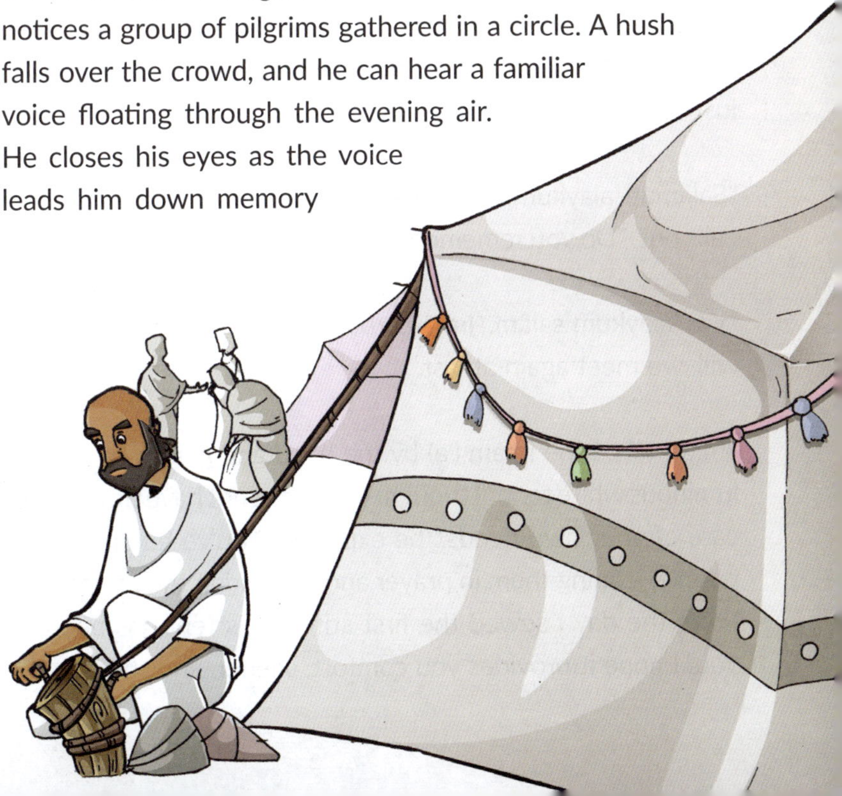

lane to the last time he was at the side of his beloved Imām (ʿa). A tear leaks out from behind his closed lids. After all these years...

ʿImrān opens his eyes and walks purposefully toward his tent. Lovingly, he takes his gift out from his bag and fingers the careful stitches. After all these years of waiting, it is time to give the gift to the person it was made for. Working swiftly and skillfully with his hands, ʿImrān sets up the tent he has brought for the Imām (ʿa)—tall, white, and luminous beneath the moon and stars. Then he waits. Once the crowd disperses, he approaches the Imām (ʿa). His hands, so steady just moments before, tremble.

"Salāmun ʿalaykum, O grandson of the Messenger of Allah!" he calls out. "Do you remember your old student?"

"Wa ʿalaykum salām, ʿImrān," the Imām (ʿa) replies. "By Allah's will, we meet again at last."

ʿImrān takes the Imām (ʿa) by the hand and guides him to the luminous white tent. "I thought you might not have time to take care of your own needs," he explains. "You've been with the people, leading them in prayer and answering their questions. From the day I sewed the first stitch, this tent has been for you. I hope it provides you comfort, shelter, and shade."

“It is a beautifully made tent,” says the Imām (ʿa) as he feels the texture of the canvas flap. “If you are selling it, I’d like to buy it from you.”

“My Imām, accept it as a gift from me and my family. Just being with you again is enough reward.”

The Imām (ʿa) smiles. “May you enjoy the cover of Allah’s kindness on the day when there is no shelter except His cooling shade.”

Master and student enter the tent and sit across from each other on the simple rug spread on the ground. Their separation is over; they are together again. Late into the night, they are deep in conversation. ʿImrān clings to every word that leaves the Imām’s lips. Thirstily, he absorbs whatever wisdom he

can. For this little window in time, he is by the Imām's side once again. It is a special opportunity he may not get again for a long time, so he doesn't want to waste it.

The bustle of pilgrims continues outside until all of Mina is sleeping. ʿImrān is in bliss at Imām Ṣādiq's side. His tired body is energized. His spirit is refreshed. His love for the Imām (ʿa) is stronger than ever before. From this brief visit—this ziyārah—ʿImrān gathers the courage and inspiration he needs to fulfill the rites of the next day and face everything else that lies ahead.

Epilogue

It is the 9th of Dhul Ḥijjah. You gaze out across the plains of ʿArafāt, which are dotted with worshippers dressed in white. Your whole body tingles with excitement and anticipation. You are here on the spiritual journey of a lifetime, performing Ḥajj for the pleasure of Allah.

But that is not all. Know that the Imām of your time (ʿaj) is out there, somewhere on these plains. Know that Imām Mahdī (ʿaj) must be close. Pray to Allah with all your heart for this Ḥajj to double in blessings and become an act of ziyārah as well—ziyārah of the 12th Imām (ʿaj). This is a chance to meet him in person, face to face, on the plains of ʿArafāt, on the day of ʿArafah, just as ʿImrān ibn ʿAbdullāh met the Imām of his time, centuries ago.

Hold fast to this hope of meeting Imām Mahdī (ʿaj). Let it burn bright like a candle in the depths of your heart. Even if your prayer is not granted today, do not give up hope. Be a good Muslim, a good Shīʿah. Do what Allah and His Prophet (ṣ) ask of you. Follow in the footsteps of the Prophets and Imāms. Try to be like them in whatever way you can, standing up for what is right and against what is wrong. And, inshāʾAllāh, you will be counted among Imām Mahdī's visitors, helpers, and friends.

CHAPTER 7

Brothers in Faith

ʿAmmār ibn ʿAbd al-Ḥamīd

It is a chilly winter evening in the city of Sistan. ʿAmmār bows his head as he walks against the wind toward home. Despite his numb lips, he whispers, over and over again, "Alḥamdulillāh." It has been a good day. It always makes him happy to see his Qurʾān students shine in their studies. Opening a school for teaching children Qurʾān has been one of the most rewarding decisions of his life. The warmth and gratitude he feels inside counters the icy wind against his skin.

When he reaches home, he ducks into the stables to check on his horses before going inside. Even they seem to feel the chill. Both horses are huddled together in one corner, using one another as blankets to keep warm. ʿAmmār smiles and reaches up to a shelf to pull down two thick woolen blankets, almost like rugs. He lays the blankets over the two horses and then leaves the stables, closing the door quietly behind him.

Inside his home, the embers are still smoldering in the fireplace from the morning. He adds in some more logs and stokes the fire until it roars to life. Then he settles down near the hearth for a simple meal of bread and dates, gazing into the flames as he eats, deep in thought.

No matter what time of day, his mind always ends up taking him to thoughts of his Imām, Imām Ṣādiq (ʿa). A tiny voice in the back of his head whispers, When will we see him next?

There is a sudden knocking at the door. "I wasn't expecting any visitors," ʿAmmār says aloud. He stands up, walks to the door, and opens it.

"ʿAbdullāh!" he exclaims. "Salāmun ʿalaykum! What are you doing here so late?" He gestures to ʿAbdullāh to come inside and closes the door behind him. "Come and warm yourself up by the fire. Would you like anything to eat?"

"Wa ʿalaykum salām, ʿAmmār," ʿAbdullāh says, smiling, as they both sit down before the fireplace. "Nothing's wrong. Don't worry about me; I've already eaten. I just wanted to drop by. I was thinking about you earlier, and I wanted to see you."

ʿAmmār studies ʿAbdullāh's face. He knows that ʿAbdullāh has been struggling with his faith for a long time. ʿAbdullāh is a lively friend with a good sense of humor and a charming smile, but there are times when he laughs even about things that are serious, making it all a big joke. Because of this, ʿAmmār is often worried about his friend. But this time, ʿAmmār notices that something has changed in his friend's wide smile.

"You can be honest with me, ʿAbdullāh," ʿAmmār says. "I know you're here for something more than that. What's on your mind?"

ʿAbdullāh smiles again, but there is the slightest hint of sadness behind that smile. "Somehow you always seem to know what's going on in people's heads. ʿAmmār, you don't know how much I wish I could be more like you—how much I wish I had your intelligence!"

As ʿAbdullāh speaks, ʿAmmār stands up to bring him some water. "ʿAbdullāh," he says, "faith is so much more important than intelligence. Intelligence is no good if you don't know how to use it. I struggle with that every day."

There is a pause in the conversation. ʿAmmār thinks back to all the times when he wanted to talk about faith with his friend, but was too afraid that such a conversation would damage their friendship—all the times he wished he could get to know ʿAbdullāh better, but just didn't know how to ask the right questions.

Now, he realizes that avoiding ʿAbdullāh might not have been the best thing to do. All these years, ʿAmmār has been afraid that ʿAbdullāh would be a bad influence on him, but maybe this is a chance to turn things the other way around. This might be an opportunity for ʿAmmār to be a positive influence on ʿAbdullāh—to strengthen him in belief and show him a better way of life.

"So tell me," ʿAmmār asks gently, "Why did you come?"

ʿAbdullāh looks ʿAmmār in the eyes and says, "ʿAmmār, I want to go for *ʿumrah* and visit the house of Allah."

"That's wonderful!" ʿAmmār says, taking care to conceal his surprise. ʿAbdullāh has never expressed any desire to visit Mecca before, but it seems that he is a changed man.

"I want us both to go," ʿAbdullāh continues. "I know you are right when you say faith is more important than intelligence. If I go, maybe I will change. Maybe I can make up for my past mistakes."

"May Allah accept your sincere efforts," ʿAmmār says, beaming. "Inshāʾ Allāh this pilgrimage will bring you many blessings. Never doubt Allah. He never abandons anyone who trusts in Him."

"So, will you come with me?" ʿAbdullāh asks.

"Of course I'll come with you!" ʿAmmār replies, and the two friends embrace like brothers.

The following week, ʿAmmār and ʿAbdullāh join a caravan that is headed toward Mecca. From the moment they depart until the time they arrive, they are engrossed in deep conversations with each other as they share their goals and aspirations for this spiritual journey.

"The thought of walking where Prophet Ibrāhīm, Prophet Ismāʿīl, and Lady Hājar (ʿa) once walked fills me with awe," ʿAbdullāh confesses. "I would give anything to be able to follow in their footsteps—to be able to see their footsteps! Sometimes I just don't think I'm worthy of such an honor."

When he sees the footprints embedded in stone at Maqām Ibrāhīm, he is speechless. Between Ṣafā and Marwah, he can see, in his mind's eye, Lady Hājar's frantic footprints tracing seven paths through the sand. At the well of Zamzam, he can just picture Prophet Ismāʿīl's little feet thrashing until clear water gushes forth.

"Now, I have seen their footprints," ʿAbdullāh says to ʿAmmār once their ʿumrah is complete, "and I pray I am able to follow them."

Before heading home, the two friends decide to travel to Medina to perform ziyārah of Prophet Muḥammad (ṣ), Sayyidah Fāṭimah, Imām Ḥasan, Imām Sajjād, and Imām Bāqir (ʿa). After spending a few days in the Prophet's Mosque and

among the graves in Jannat al-Baqīʿ, ʿAbdullāh asks, "Now that we've finished our ziyārah, are we going to go home?"

"We retraced the footsteps of Prophet Ibrāhīm (ʿa) and his family when we visited the House of Allah," ʿAmmār replies. "We visited the graves of so many great personalities who are no longer with us on this earth. But the legacy of Prophet Ibrāhīm (ʿa) and the Ahl al-Bayt (ʿa) is still alive—right here, in Medina. It lives on in our Imām, Jaʿfar aṣ-Ṣādiq (ʿa). So we have one more stop to make before we turn back." ʿAmmār clasps ʿAbdullāh's hand. "Come with me to visit him. I know he wants to meet you."

"Why would he want to meet me? I'm nobody," ʿAbdullāh says, confused. "I've made so many mistakes. I'm too ashamed to meet him."

"I spoke with him when we first arrived, when you had gone to visit your friend. He greeted me, and then the first question he asked was 'Where is your friend, ʿAbdullāh? I've been waiting to meet him.' He really wants to see you," ʿAmmār replies in earnest. "Please, let me take you to Imām Ṣādiq (ʿa). When we feel lost, he is the one who can guide us."

"Alright. I'll come with you."

ʿAmmār smiles. "Good. We still have a little while until Maghrib. If we hurry, we'll make it there just in time."

Waiting on the Imām's doorstep, ʿAbdullāh is restless. ʿAmmār places a reassuring hand on his shoulder. "This is the moment you've been waiting for. I know you're ready." At that moment, the door opens, and the Imām (ʿa) steps out to meet them.

"Salāmun ʿalaykum," he says with a warm smile. "ʿAmmār, it is good to see you again. ʿAbdullāh, welcome—I have been waiting to meet you!" The Imām (ʿa) greets and embraces ʿAbdullāh like an old friend before inviting him inside, guiding him by the hand.

After introductions are over, ʿAmmār slips out of the room to give ʿAbdullāh some time alone with the Imām (ʿa). He knows that a one-on-one conversation with the Imām is enough to change someone's life forever. He watches the light fade near the western horizon and watches the redness of the sun's reflection slowly creep across the sky until it hangs overhead. In the distance, he hears the muʾadhdhin begin reciting the adhān.

Before long, ʿAbdullāh steps out of the house, his face transformed by a look of hope. "Thank you for bringing me to meet our Imām (ʿa)," he says. "I used to think that Allah wouldn't want me because of all my mistakes, but now I realize that the door to repentance is always open, and that it's never too late to turn toward Allah if you are sincere. And now I see that Allah hasn't left us alone; we have guides like the Imāms (ʿa) who can help us find the right path again when we lose our way."

The sound of the adhān floats across the city as the sky deepens from cobalt blue to indigo to velvety violet. The Imām (ʿa) soon joins them outside, and the brothers in faith walk toward the Prophet's Mosque for Maghrib prayers. Every step brings them closer to Allah.

Epilogue

Though we cannot see and hear our Imāms (ʿa), they can still see and hear us. They hear us when we call out their names and when we perform their ziyārah. They see our every action, both the good deeds and the bad. They are constantly praying for their Shīʿah. They have never abandoned us, even if we sometimes forget about them.

If we truly, sincerely try to follow them, then, with Allah's permission, they can take us by the hand, guide us through the trials of the Day of Judgment, and lead us to Jannah. When we recite Duʿā Tawassul, we are asking them for this special favor. Through the duʿās that they have taught us, we can speak with Allah using their words, and we become closer to them and closer to the Lord we all serve.

CHAPTER 8

Two Letters

ʿAbdullāh ibn an-Najāshī

Long green palm fronds wave like fingers in the hot wind. Dates hang in bunches like glistening black pearls. ʿAbdullāh sighs and leans back against a palm trunk, gazing up into the bits of sky that peek through the leaves, a letter clenched in his right hand. Then he continues his agitated pacing along the palm tree shadow that stretches across the sun-baked earth.

The soldier who was sent as a messenger stands by, awaiting further orders. After a while, ʿAbdullāh still has not spoken a word. "What message should I take back to the khalīfah?" asks the soldier.

ʿAbdullāh stays silent. With his left hand, he grips his beard. His brow is furrowed with worry. Again, the soldier asks, "What are your orders? Do you have a message for the khalīfah?"

Distractedly, ʿAbdullāh replies, "No—I don't have an answer yet. I need some time before I can make a decision."

Once the soldier leaves, ʿAbdullāh stops pacing and rests his head against the palm trunk, gazing up at the bunches of dates that sway gently in the wind.

The contents of the letter churn in his mind. His right fist tightens around the letter, crumpling it into a ball. The letter contains the khalīfah's request for ʿAbdullāh to accept the governorship of Ahvaz. ʿAbdullāh does not know whether to feel angry or honored. The khalīfah is a cruel and unjust ruler who cares little about his people. There is no way ʿAbdullāh would want to be part of such an evil regime. Yet, at the same time, this may be an opportunity for ʿAbdullāh to take charge and change things for the better. Should he accept the offer?

ʿAbdullāh is blessed with a good life and a good family. The people around him love and respect him. He helps the poor find ways to earn money when the khalīfah denies them help. What will they say if he becomes part of the government that has done so much to oppress them? Will their goodwill turn to hatred and resentment?

ʿAbdullāh clenches the crumpled letter and bites his lip. Even if the way the people see him does not change, what about his Imām (ʿa)? What will Imām Ṣādiq (ʿa) think when he sees his loyal follower serving a man whose forefathers have shed so much of the Ahl al-Bayt's blood?

He throws the letter on the ground. He wants no part in it! Not if it means he loses the love and respect of his Imām (ʿa). He wants no part in an evil, corrupt government.

But what if he is the one who can help make it good?

He runs his hands over his face and then brings them together in duʿā. "O Allah," he whispers, "I beg You to help me, guide me. Help me choose what pleases You, not me."

He gathers his thoughts, picks up the letter from the ground, and begins to walk toward his home. With each step, he feels calmer. He considers his options. As much as he wants to burn the letter and watch it be devoured by angry flames, he knows that he will have to answer to the khalīfah. The khalīfah's requests are not something that can be taken lightly, and burning the letter would be a rash and dangerous thing to do. Instead, ʿAbdullāh decides that, once he gets home, he will lock the letter away in a chest until he knows what to do.

Although being home brings him some comfort and relief, ʿAbdullāh's anger still boils beneath the surface. It is hard to think clearly, and the longer he tries to hide his emotions, the harder it becomes to see beyond the darkness that threatens to swallow him. He is haunted by an image of him becoming an enemy of the Imām (ʿa) and the Shīʿah. He can hear his wife calling him for dinner, but it sounds like she is talking from very far away. She comes closer and sits next to him and takes him by the hand.

"ʿAbdullāh, you look upset. Can you tell me what's wrong?" she asks.

"I'm sorry—I don't feel very hungry. I think I need some time alone."

"Maybe talking about it will help," she suggests.

"I saw you come in with that letter, and I watched you lock it away. I know it's bothering you."

"I just don't know what to think or what to say. I feel trapped," he says.

"Maybe I can't help you, but I know someone who can—someone you can talk to, and He will always listen and understand." She squeezes his hand and stands up. "Dinner is ready whenever you are."

ʿAbdullāh nods and decides to take her advice. Though he has already prayed Maghrib and ʿIshāʾ, he lays out his prayer rug, curls into sajdah, and begins to speak with the One who always listens. In that position, forehead pressed against his turbah, he feels the weight of the letter on his shoulders. At the same time, all his doubts and worries come back to flood his mind, and he lets them all out in a whispered stream of prayer. Tears leak out from the corners of his eyes and pool around the turbah as he begs Allah for the strength to make the right choice.

Even after seeking Allah's help, that night, ʿAbdullāh still struggles to sleep. He knows his job is not done. He has taken the first step—seeking help from Allah—but he cannot stop there and wait for a solution to appear from the sky. He still needs to do his part. Who can he ask who knows best what Allah would want?

Then it occurs to him. Why not ask Imām Ṣādiq (ʿa) himself? It's the perfect solution. If he explains the situation, then he can see what the Imām (ʿa) recommends. He promises himself and Allah that he will do whatever the Imām (ʿa) thinks best. He decides to write a letter first thing tomorrow morning and is finally able to fall asleep.

Once the letter is sent, ʿAbdullāh can do nothing but wait. He carries out his daily duties and goes to the homes of those families in his community he knows need help, but he tries to stay away from open, public spaces. He knows that the khalīfah will be impatiently awaiting his response, and he doesn't want to risk being cornered by a messenger—or worse, a soldier—and put his family in danger by giving the khalīfah an answer that makes him angry.

At last, the Imām's answer comes. Eagerly, ʿAbdullāh opens the letter and reads it together with his wife:

In the name of Allah, the All-Beneficent, the All-Merciful

Salāmun ʿalaykum dearest ʿAbdullāh,

It gladdens me to know that you have been offered the governorship of Ahvaz. I have faith in the goodness and piety of your heart, and I know that you will use whatever power you gain to continue helping the poor, the needy, and the lovers of the Ahl al-Bayt, just as you always have. You may even be able to guide the wretched to what is good and help them find their way to the right path. This is your chance to do what you can to free the Shīʿah of the Ahl al-Bayt from the oppression they have suffered at the hands of false and corrupt governments.

ʿAbdullāh sighs with relief. At the same time, he feels the weight of the responsibility that the Imām (ʿa) is entrusting him with. Will he be able to live up to those great expectations? The last line from the letter is a grave warning:

Remember that if you ever use this position for evil—to steal the rights of others for your own benefit—you will never smell the fragrance of Heaven.

Was salām

ʿAbdullāh breathes deeply. With his wife as his witness, he vows, "I swear by Allah that my Imām (ʿa) is right. I will accept the khalīfah's offer, not for personal gain, but to help my people and to please Allah."

Epilogue

ʿAbdullāh watches from a distance as a group of young boys chase each other in the shade of an orchard of date palms. When they are tired of their play, they gather their baskets full of dates to take home for their families. As governor of Ahvaz, ʿAbdullāh has worked to make sure that all people living in the city receive their fair share of provisions. He encourages the wealthy to look out for their neighbors, and encourages even the poor to share what they have with others. With Allah's help and the Imām's advice, he has been able to make Ahvaz a more just and God-conscious society.

CHAPTER 9

A Gift for a Gift

Muḥammad ibn ʿAlī an-Naysābūrī

There is a great hustle and bustle in the town square. People gather around the long train of camels, which are laden with gifts from the people of Nishapur for Imām Kāẓim (ʿa) in Medina. There are wooden chests and bundles wrapped in cloth perched between the camels' humps, and big satchels of letters hang down at the camels' sides. The animals' harnesses jangle like bells; the train is just about ready to depart.

The crowd presses in closer around the caravan, calling out to the man who stands at its head: Muḥammad ibn ʿAlī Nishapurī.

“Convey to the Imām (ʿa) my salāms!” many of them beg.

“Send my respects to my master, Imām Kāẓim (ʿa)! My life, my wealth—it is all for him.”

“May Allah help you safely reach Medina,” someone prays.

Muḥammad smiles and nods, holding his horse’s reins. His gaze sweeps over the crowd of sincere well-wishers and followers of the Imām (ʿa), and his heart swells with gratitude to Allah for granting him this opportunity to serve the Imām (ʿa) and his fellow Shīʿah once again. The people have entrusted Muḥammad with their khums—one fifth of all of the extra money and wealth that they have saved up, but do not use; and the Imām (ʿa) has entrusted him with the task of safely delivering the khums to Medina. Year after year, Muḥammad has faithfully performed this duty, and he has earned the respect of his people and his Imām (ʿa) without ever disappointing them even once.

It is an enormous responsibility. The caravan carries 30,000 gold coins and 50,000 silver coins, along with finely woven, expensive fabrics. Each person has offered what is most valuable and most dear to them as his or her gift for the Imām (ʿa).

Even the satchels filled with letters are precious, but for a different reason. Every year, along with their khums, the scholars of Nishapur write letters to the Imām (ʿa). They humbly request the Imām (ʿa) to fill the gaps and holes in their own understanding with his knowledge, and they present him with some of the questions that the people have asked, in the hopes that their whole community can benefit from the Imām's wisdom.

Muḥammad's mission is like a grand trading venture. He exchanges one load of treasure for something even more valuable: the people offer the Imām (ʿa) their gifts of fine fabrics and coins, and the Imām (ʿa) gives them the gift of knowledge and wisdom in return.

The crowd continues to buzz with prayers and requests. Some weep because they cannot meet the Imām (ʿa) in person; Muḥammad does his best to comfort them and promises that he will send salāms to the Imām (ʿa) on their behalf. Along with their gifts and questions, he bears the responsibility of representing them before their Imām (ʿa) and bringing their hearts closer to the Imām (ʿa), despite the vast distance that stretches between Medina and Nishapur.

After saying his final farewells, Muḥammad mounts his horse. He is just about to signal to the men who will be his helpers on this journey to begin moving forward when an old woman grabs hold of his horse's reins.

"My son—wait!" she pleads. "I have a gift for my Imām

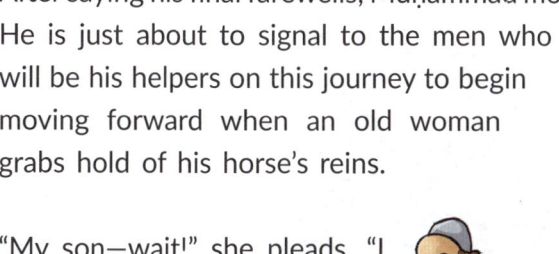

as well. Will you take it to him?" She holds out a white handkerchief and a silver coin in her palm. "I know it isn't much, but I still want to fulfill my duty to my Imām. I hope he is able to use it to help someone in need."

Muḥammad dismounts out of respect for the old woman so that he does not have to look down at her to speak to her. Her gift is simple, and a voice in the back of his mind whispers, What value could it possibly have? But he does not want to break her heart by belittling or rejecting her gift, so he smiles, and takes the handkerchief and coin from her hand. He tucks the silver coin away with some other coins, and places the handkerchief with the other fabrics.

Then, he mounts his horse again and begins to lead the caravan onward. Behind him, the people wave, and children run after the caravan to escort it out of the city. When they can no longer keep up, they stop and watch until the caravan with all its camels is a tiny speck, far away.

It takes over two months to travel from Nishapur to Medina. It is not an easy journey. Muḥammad must constantly be on the lookout for bandits. He and his helpers are always on high alert. Even worse than being attacked by bandits would be to run into any officials of the Abbasid government. If they find out that the caravan is bound for Imām Kāẓim (ʿa) in Medina, there will be serious consequences. At least bandits only care about gold and silver, but the Abbasid ruler, Hārūn, would want to punish the Imām (ʿa) and all of his supporters if he discovers Muḥammad's mission. Muḥammad takes care never to pass too close to Baghdad, the Abbasid capital, and by Allah's grace, all these years, he has never been caught. If he is, his backup

plan is to pretend he is a merchant going to Medina to buy and sell goods.

Despite the long and tiring journey, Muḥammad and his men are in high spirits. Their eagerness to see the Imām (ʿa) gives them energy. They pray to Allah to protect them from the dangers of the road and rise cheerfully to meet the challenges of each new day.

At long last, they reach Medina, safe and sound. The people of Medina are used to seeing these great khums caravans, and with their help, Muḥammad guides the caravan to Imām Kāẓim's (ʿa) house. Everyone works together to unload the cargo. When all the unloading is done, Muḥammad's helpers tend to the camels and horses, and Muḥammad enters the Imām's house to sit with him and speak with him.

"Salāmun ʿalaykum, O grandson of the Messenger of Allah!" Muḥammad says as he gently kisses the Imām's hand. "Your Shīʿah in Nishapur send their prayers and salāms as well. Their hearts are with you despite the thousands of miles of desert that separate them from you."

"Wa ʿalaykum salām, Muḥammad," the Imām (ʿa) replies. "Send my salāms to them as well. It is difficult to be so far apart from so many faithful communities. May Allah reward them for their loyalty and their faith. It isn't always easy to give in Allah's way—to pay khums and zakāh, to give ṣadaqah. Alḥamdulillāh, Allah has given them the strength to still carry out these duties." The Imām (ʿa) pauses. Then he says, "There was a lady named Āminah—will you bring me the gift that she gave? I'd like to see it."

At first, Muḥammad isn't sure what the Imām (ʿa) means. "Which lady? I don't remember anyone with that name."

"She was the one who gave the silver coin wrapped in a white handkerchief."

Muḥammad is speechless. He is awed by the Imām's miraculous knowledge and doesn't know how to respond. He realizes he did not do the old woman justice when he received her humble gift. He dismissed it as something of little worth, but now the Imām (ʿa) is singling out her gift for a unique honor. Now, Muḥammad feels ashamed before the Imām (ʿa). He doesn't know how he will find that one silver coin among 50,000 other coins, or how he will find that one square of white cloth among all the bundles of other fabrics.

The Imām (ʿa) reads Muḥammad's silence and comes to his aid. "The coin is in that red bag with 40 gold coins in it, and the handkerchief is in that green bundle, on top of the expensive woven cloth from Balkh."

Remorseful and wonderstruck, Muḥammad follows the Imām's instructions and digs out both the coin and the cloth from where he had put them for safekeeping. As they pass from his hands to the Imām's hands, the old woman's face—Āminah's face—flashes

through his mind. This time, he glimpses in her eyes the oceans of sincerity which escaped his notice before.

The Imām (ʿa) continues, "Muḥammad—give my salāms to Āminah, and tell her I am very thankful for her gift. She has fulfilled her responsibility. Even a small good deed brings lots of blessings and rewards if it is done sincerely. I have something for her as well." He stands up and disappears behind a curtain into another room. He returns with a bag filled with 40 gold coins and a length of neatly folded cloth. "My sister, Ḥalīmah, wove this cloth from the cotton that grows in my cotton field. It is a kafan, a burial shroud."

There is a moment of silence as Muḥammad realizes the meaning of the Imām's words. "Do you mean—" he starts, "do you mean it is meant to be her kafan?"

The Imām (ʿa) nods. "Āminah is not long for this world. Within 19 days of your return to Khorasan, Allah will take her soul. She has lived a faithful and sincere life, and Allah will reward her for her devotion. She spent the last of what she had in giving me that silver coin and that white handkerchief. I would like you to take this fabric as her kafan and this money to cover whatever costs she may have in the last stages of her life."

Muḥammad is silent as Imām Kāẓim (ʿa) describes for him the high status of the old woman, Āminah. Now he sees that her sincerity has made her single silver coin more valuable than the rest of the caravan's gifts combined. Since she has made pleasing Allah and the Imām (ʿa) her lifelong goal, her reward in this world is to be buried in a shroud hand-woven by Sayyidah Ḥalīmah, and her reward in the hereafter is the company of Imām Kāẓim (ʿa) and the rest of the Maʿṣūmīn (ʿa) in Paradise.

When Muḥammad returns to Khorasan after two months on the road, even before going to his own house, he knows he must pay Āminah a visit. He realizes with a jolt that he doesn't know where she lives. After an hour of searching and asking around, he finally finds his way to Āminah's house. A young boy, who Muḥammad guesses is her son, opens the door.

“Salāmun ʿalaykum,” Muḥammad says. “Is your mother home?”

“Wa ʿalaykum salām,” replies the boy. “She is home, but she is very sick. I know she will be happy to see you, though. You’re the one who takes our gifts to Imām Kāẓim (ʿa). I always love watching when your caravan leaves, with all those enormous camels.”

Muḥammad smiles. “You and your mother have hearts bigger than any camel. What is your name?”

“My name is Mūsā.” With that, Mūsā invites Muḥammad inside and leads him to Āminah’s bedside.

“Mother, dear,” Mūsā says. “We have a visitor.”

“Salāmun ʿalaykum,” Muḥammad says, kneeling beside the frail old woman. “My name is Muḥammad. I’m not sure if you remember me, but—”

Upon hearing Muḥammad’s name, Āminah slowly opens her eyes and meets his gaze.

“Alḥamdulillāh, you came back safely,” she says, her lined face crinkling into a smile.

Tears well up in Muḥammad's eyes. This old woman whose name he had not known until the Imām (ʿa) told him—whose sincere gift he had failed to appreciate—knew him by name and treated him like her own son.

"Imām Kāẓim (ʿa) sends you his salāms and thanks you for your gift," Muḥammad says. "He sent you some gifts as well." He lays the kafan by her arm so she can feel it.

"It's beautiful," she murmurs.

"It is from the Imām (ʿa) and his sister, Sayyidah Ḥalīmah (ʿa)."

They are silent for a moment. Muḥammad looks around to see if Mūsā is still nearby. He does not know how to continue with the rest of the Imām's tidings.

"Inshāʾallāh, I can use it for my burial shroud," Āminah continues in a soft half-whisper. "I did not have anything for a kafan before. I'm sure the Imām (ʿa) must have known this. It is very kind of him to send one."

By now, Muḥammad's cheeks are wet. He can see the light radiating from every crevice of Āminah's face.

"Please, tell me if there is anything you need, anything I can do for you or for Mūsā," he says earnestly. "You've treated me like a son; let me treat you like a mother."

"Thank you, Muḥammad. You've brought joy and happiness to my heart. My only request is that you look after Mūsā and teach him and guide him. May Allah grant both of you long lives, so you can continue to serve our master, Imām Kāẓim (ʿa)."

Then, Āminah falls silent. Muḥammad can sense Mūsā standing in the doorway behind him, watching and listening. He stands up and turns around, and he sees the tears glistening in Mūsā's eyes. They look at each other without speaking for a long moment before Muḥammad wraps Mūsā in a hug, both of them shaking with sobs.

CHAPTER 10

Barefoot Rich Man

Bishr ibn al-Ḥārith al-Ḥāfī

Prologue

A little boy lies with his head in his mother's lap as she raises her hands in duʿā. He blinks sleepily in the flickering candlelight and lets his mother's voice wash over him.

"O Allah! I am so very grateful that You have guided me and my family to be Shīʿah of the Imāms (ʿa). Help us show our loyalty to them by always following in their footsteps and always being by their side. Help me raise my children to serve their Imāms in whatever way they can. If they ever stray from the right path, help them find their way back to You through Your Imāms!"

As he drifts off to sleep, the little boy can hear his mother speaking softly to him.

"Dearest Bishr—remember which masters you serve. You are a servant to your Lord, Allah. You are a servant to the children of ʿAlī (ʿa) and Fāṭimah (ʿa). Don't let the toys of this world distract you with their sparkle and their glitter. Don't dig for treasure in places that take you far away from your Lord. The best treasures are with Allah and His Imāms (ʿa)."

"Why are you already packing your bags? Are you going back to Baghdad again?" Laylā folds her arms and looks unhappily at her husband.

"I need to take care of some unfinished business," Bishr says without looking her in the eye. "I'll be back soon, and I'll bring even more presents for you and the children. Don't worry."

"I don't like it when you go so far away from us. Your home is here. What is it about Baghdad that takes you away from us so often? We love to have you here with us. When you come back, you are always changed, and you act strange, like you don't even know your own family."

Bishr says nothing for a moment. Images of Baghdad's wide boulevards, courtyards,

fountains, and enormous markets flash through his mind, and he feels a twinge of guilt that he is not being completely honest with his wife.

"I need to go," he repeats, cutting the conversation short. "I promise I'll be back soon."

Laylā sighs. She knows he is hiding something; he never likes to share what exactly his business in Baghdad is. She can only pray with all her heart that he does not forget his roots and his values when he's all alone.

"Alright. Just don't forget that when you feel lonely, Allah is still with you. Inshā'Allāh you go and come safely. Who knows, you may even catch a glimpse of our beloved Imām Kāẓim ('a)." She manages a smile and forces Bishr to meet her gaze. He looks at her for a moment and then looks away, shifting his feet uncomfortably.

Bishr and his family live in Merv, a beautiful, fair-weathered city in the province of Khorasan. But Bishr is often away on "business" trips and disappears to faraway places. Each time, he returns with more goods, more wealth, and more presents for his wife and children; but he is never at peace when he is home. He is restless, and speaks very little, and often escapes again within a few weeks—usually to Baghdad, which is almost 900 miles away.

Once he is in Baghdad, he is free; he does not have to meet Laylā's worried, concerned gaze. He does not have to try and explain himself to her and come up with excuses. He does not have to constantly feel guilty, like he is doing something wrong, something that she will not like, something that might sadden and disappoint her if she finds out.

Baghdad is a magnificent city, with great circular outer walls and four big gates. It is the capital of the Abbasid rulers. Inside, the city walkways are lined with shops and bazaars. The streets are always bustling with travelers visiting from various countries: scholars, merchants, and businessmen like Bishr. Here, Bishr loses himself in the crowds and wanders wherever he pleases. He even has his own house for when he visits for longer periods of time, like now.

When night falls, sleep is far from Bishr's mind. He decides to invite some of his friends, acquaintances, and fellow businessmen to his house. He has his servants work round the clock to prepare dishes of roast meat and saffron rice, as well as jugs of wine for each night's festivities. Late into the night, Bishr and his guests can be heard laughing, playing and listening to music, and having a good time, throwing all their worries and responsibilities behind them.

At the same time that Bishr is in Baghdad, so is Imām Kāẓim (ʿa). The Abbasid tyrant Hārūn had the Imām (ʿa) brought from Medina by force so that he could keep an eye on him. Some days, he confines the Imām (ʿa) in prison; other days, he sets the Imām (ʿa) free, though the city, with its massive walls, is its own kind of prison.

One night, when the Imām (ʿa) is free to wander the greater of the two prisons, he passes by Bishr's house while a party is underway. A strain of loud, raucous music bursts out from an open window. The Imām (ʿa) pauses in the otherwise quiet street. Within a couple of minutes, Bishr's door opens, and a servant hurries out with a bucket of food scraps and other garbage.

"Salāmun ʿalaykum," the Imām (ʿa) greets her from the street.

"Wa ʿalaykum salām," the servant replies, peering into the darkness to see who it is.

The Imām (ʿa) approaches the doorstep, stepping into the light cast by the open door. In a concerned voice, he asks, "What is happening here? Is everything alright? Who is the owner of this house? Is he wealthy or in need?"

When she recognizes the Imām (ʿa), the servant respectfully replies, "He is a wealthy man, O grandson of Allah's Messenger. He is not needy."

The Imām (ʿa) nods slowly. "You must be right. He cannot be a needy man. If he was in need of Allah, he would not be doing what he is doing." He looks at the servant, and with a courteous, "Was salām," he continues on his way.

The servant remains on the doorstep for a moment before returning inside. She can sense the Imām's disapproval despite his calm tone. It weighs heavily on her mind. She feels uneasy about being involved in something that displeases her Imām (ʿa).

When she reenters the house, Bishr impatiently calls out,

"What took you so long? Come quickly! My guests are thirsty, and they need their cups refilled."

As the servant bends to pour them drinks, she murmurs softly to Bishr, "My master! Imām Kāẓim (ʿa) just passed me on the street. He asked me if the owner of this house was rich or needy. I told him: 'He is not needy.' He replied: 'You must be right—if he was in need of Allah, he would not be doing what he is doing...'"

Bishr's hand begins to tremble uncontrollably. His glass slips from between his fingers and shatters to pieces on the floor. He is so overcome by the Imām's words that the color drains from his face and he becomes deathly pale.

"Enough!" he shouts hoarsely. The laughter and music stops. He staggers to his feet, rushes to the door and out onto

the street. Rocks and gravel bite into his bare feet as he runs in the direction of his Imām (ʿa).

Allah's name is on his lips as he runs. "Forgive me, my Lord; forgive me," he gasps, breathing in jagged bursts. "Master!" he cries out, "Please, wait!"

The Imām (ʿa) turns around and sees Bishr—barefoot, panting, tears streaming down his face. Bishr falls to his knees and kisses the Imām's hand. "Forgive me," he repeats brokenly. "I beg Allah to forgive me; I beg you to beg Allah to forgive me. You've made me realize my sins!

The Imām (ʿa) takes Bishr's hand and helps him to stand up. He looks kindly at Bishr and says, "Allah will forgive you if your repentance is sincere. If you make every effort to change your ways, Allah will continue to guide you out from the dark and into the light. Listen to the voices of truth and conscience around you—your mother, your wife, your children."

Bishr nods gratefully, but still hangs his head with shame.

The Imām (ʿa) continues, "And if you are ever tempted by the toys of this world, with their sparkle and glitter, remember Allah is with you, and Allah is watching. See how you can serve Him and please Him. He is your master, not this world. Inshā'Allah He will give you strength to continue to serve and please Him."

"Please, tell me what I can do to serve and please Him. Where can I start?" Bishr asks humbly.

"Start with your family. Spend time with your wife and children. Show them your love and affection. Help raise your children like your mother raised you—to love goodness and to know right from wrong."

"Thank you," Bishr says. "You've given me a new life."

After a final exchange of salāms, he and the Imām (ʿa) part ways. Bishr returns to his house, barefoot. It is empty. The guests have all left in a hurry. Bishr sighs, relieved. He helps the servants clean up after all his merrymaking. He decides that the next morning, he will set out for home.

For so long, his heart has been uneasy and discontent. For so long, he has tried to hide his guilt. Now, he realizes what he has been doing wrong, and he promises himself and Allah that he will not repeat his mistakes. Now, at last, he feels at peace.

For the first time in a long time, instead of dreading his return, Bishr is eager to be home. As he approaches his house, he sees his children playing on the street with other children. Laylā stands by the door, smiling at their antics. He slowly walks toward her until she notices, and her smile widens.

"Salāmun ʿalaykum—you're home!" she exclaims, throwing her arms around him in a big hug. Then she looks at him for a long moment. "It's so good to see you, looking happy like this."

Bishr knows the question that must be on her mind: what happened? He decides to answer it before she even asks.

"Wa ʿalaykum salām—I'm glad to be home. I met our Imām Kāẓim (ʿa), and he helped me see how badly I've been acting, especially toward you and the children. I'm truly sorry, and I hope I can make it up to you," Bishr explains. "Thank you for always being there for me and never giving up on me," he adds shyly.

"Alḥamdulillāh! Allah has fulfilled my prayers in the best way," Laylā says, smiling through happy tears, as the children see their father is home and welcome him with hugs and kisses.

Epilogue

While making sure to spend plenty of time with his family in Merv, Bishr continues his trips to Baghdad—this time with the purpose of strengthening his connection with Imām Kāẓim (ʿa). He comes to be known as Bishr al-Ḥāfī, Bishr "the Barefoot." He shows the sincerity of his repentance by turning away from his past mistakes and toward Allah. He becomes a loving husband, a caring father, and one of Imām Kāẓim's greatest companions.

CHAPTER 11

Rain and Tears

Ibrāhīm ibn Muḥammad

A light sprinkling of rain cools the streets of Khorasan as Ibrāhīm walks toward the masjid for Friday prayers. Ibrāhīm loves the feel of rain on his skin; he has learned from his Imāms (ʿa) that rain is Allah's way of showering the world with His mercy. He tucks his book under his cloak to protect it. It will be difficult to give the khuṭbah without his notes!

After the muʾadhdhin gives the adhān, Ibrāhīm ascends the pulpit and begins his Friday sermon. Every face is turned eagerly toward him, ready to hear whatever wisdom he has to offer. The people know Ibrāhīm for his powerful sermons, which overflow with the teachings of the Imāms (ʿa). His gentle voice washes over the crowd as it carries the words of the Imāms (ʿa) to every listener's heart. Every now and then, a pair of eyes sparkles with tears, or a teardrop traces its way down someone's cheek.

As Ibrāhīm speaks, people in the gathering begin to hear the clatter of hoofbeats approaching the masjid from

outside. They hear a harsh voice barking orders. Suddenly, a group of soldiers bursts through the back doors of the masjid. The commander's voice rings out across the neat rows of worshippers as he bellows, "That's him—arrest him at once!"

The soldiers jab their way through the crowd, unashamed of using their boots to shove people aside. Two of them climb the pulpit, and each grabs hold of one of Ibrāhīm's arms. They drag him down from the pulpit and tie his hands before weaving their way through the masjid and the worshippers assembled in it.

The whole masjid is in an uproar. The worshippers scramble to their feet and face the soldiers, fighting to free Ibrāhīm. One man grasps Ibrāhīm's bound hands and tries elbowing the guards to force them to let go. The people are just about to overpower the first band of soldiers sent into the masjid when the commander sends in a second wave. The soldiers are ruthless. They do not hold back. They form a ring around Ibrāhīm and his captors and threateningly flail long whips at those attacking them. When the people still do not give up, the soldiers lash out at children and grown men alike. Once they carry Ibrāhīm outside, they hoist him onto a horse, and the commander gallops away at full speed with Ibrāhīm in tow while the soldiers finish fending off the enraged crowd.

Now, the masjid is quiet again. The crowd is devastated. They have failed to save their wise teacher from the clutches of the Abbasid khalīfah, Hārūn, and his soldiers. One man holds a bound stack of papers tightly in his hand: Ibrāhīm's notes—his handwritten record of some teachings and ḥadīth from the Imāms (ʿa). The man presses the papers to his chest as tears leak out from the corners of his eyes. This is all he has left of his teacher, Ibrāhīm. This is all he was able to save from the soldiers' iron grip. He promises himself that he will keep it safe, and that the khalīfah will never lay his hands on it. It is the least he can do.

Ibrāhīm is now the khalīfah's prisoner, who punishes him savagely for his speeches from the pulpit. Even though he has only ever called the people toward goodness and truth, the khalīfah sees him as a criminal because of his love for the Imāms (ʿa). He is beaten severely by the prison guards and is not given enough food. However, he astonishes all the guards and the khalīfah himself by never complaining even once. He praises Allah and recites dhikr over and over again. He is so used to fasting that the little food he is fed is enough to satisfy his hunger.

Ibrāhīm's endurance only makes the khalīfah even more angry. The khalīfah wants to execute Ibrāhīm and be rid of him, but Ibrāhīm has committed no crime. There are no charges brought against him. The khalīfah has no good reason to execute him, but that doesn't stop him from wanting Ibrāhīm dead. He vows to catch Ibrāhīm red-handed, involved in some wrongdoing. And so he hatches a plan.

The khalīfah hires a spy and sends him into prison to be Ibrāhīm's prison mate. He tells the spy to report Ibrāhīm's every move, his every word. He is confident that it will only be a matter of time before Ibrāhīm's tongue slips and he says something against the khalīfah. If his spy can catch Ibrāhīm speaking badly about the government, then the khalīfah might have enough grounds to execute him.

However, Ibrāhīm continues to devote all his efforts to fasting and prayer. He never stops thanking Allah and expressing his gratitude. He finds strength in remembering the plight of his beloved Imām Kāẓim (ʿa), suffering in prison at the hands of the same tyrant khalīfah Hārūn in Baghdad. Years pass, and the khalīfah's cruel plots never succeed. He is never able to kill Ibrāhīm. He dies while Ibrāhīm is still in prison—innocent, blameless, and pure.

When Hārūn's son, Maʾmūn, comes into power, Ibrāhīm is finally released from prison. Darkness settles across the city as he limps home. The streets are oddly silent. His legs ache, and he keeps rubbing his wrists, which are sore after years of being in shackles. However, his first thought is not of his pain, but of his Imām (ʿa), and of gratitude to Allah for allowing him to go free at last.

As Ibrāhīm nears his street, he finds himself disoriented, and the darkness makes it even harder to see. His neighborhood looks different. There are some new, unfamiliar buildings, and some buildings that used to be there seem to be missing. Ibrāhīm's gaze shifts from one home to the next as he searches for his own. Then he spots it. A couple more houses down, there is a raised rectangle of a crumbling mud-brick wall. The roof has collapsed, and much of the front door has rotted away. The only recognizable feature is a small grove of pomegranate trees, but even those have wasted away, crowned with withered leaves and shrivelled fruit. It is clear that they have not been looked after all these years, and they are on the verge of death.

Ibrāhīm tiredly places his palm against one of the tree trunks and thanks Allah for bringing him safely home. He knows that Allah is the manager and restorer of all things. Just as He has the power to set an aging prisoner free, He has the power to rebuild ruined houses and nurse dying fruit trees back to life.

Just then, Ibrāhīm hears a door open, and someone steps out from one of the nearby houses. The man looks vaguely familiar. His gaze sweeps the street and then falls upon Ibrāhīm. He utters a small cry and hurries toward Ibrāhīm.

"Shaykh Ibrāhīm! Shaykh Ibrāhīm—is it really you? Alḥamdulillāh! You are back. All these years… we didn't know if you were alive or dead. We didn't know what they might have done to you!" He glances at what is left of Ibrāhīm's home, and then takes Ibrāhīm's hand in his own. "Please, let my family host you. Our home is your home."

"Thank you for your kindness and generosity," Ibrāhīm replies. "I'm sorry, but I don't remember your name."

"My name is Nāṣir, Shaykh. I don't think we have ever met before, but I remember your beautiful sermons very well. We all remember, and we have all missed you very much."

As they walk together toward Nāṣir's home, Ibrāhīm asks, "I don't know anything about what has happened in the outside world all these years. How is our beloved Imām Kāẓim ('a)?"

Nāṣir stops in his tracks and turns toward Ibrāhīm. Ibrāhīm can see the sorrow in his eyes, and knows what Nāṣir is about to say a split second before it is said. "He is no longer with us; he has left this world to meet his Lord. He was poisoned in Baghdad shortly after you were imprisoned."

"Surely we are from Allah, and to Him we shall return,"[1] Ibrāhīm whispers. Tears trickle down his face, and his shoulders shake with sobs. Still, he does not complain. Instead, he recites Allah's name and begs through his tears to be given the honor of meeting the martyred Imām's successor.

Nāṣir places a hand on Ibrāhīm's shoulder to console him, and the two loyal followers of the Imāms ('a) grieve together for a few moments in the darkness of night on an otherwise silent street.

Nāṣir opens up his home to Ibrāhīm and shares with him all he has. Right after the night of Ibrāhīm's return, Nāṣir reveals a buried treasure. He takes Ibrāhīm to a large wooden

1 Noble Qur'ān, 2:156

chest stored safely in a corner and presents it to him as a gift. Ibrāhīm opens the chest to find all of his writings and collections of ḥadīth, intact and unharmed. At the very top sits the bound stack of papers from which he had recited some ḥadīth during that fateful Friday sermon.

"My father rescued your book that day you were arrested," Nāṣir explains. "He was so upset that he had been unable to rescue you, and so he vowed to guard your books and writings with his life. I remember helping him carry all these papers out of your house and storing them away here. Just a few days later, we watched soldiers come and search your house. Of course, they returned to the khalīfah empty-handed."

Ibrāhīm kneels beside the chest and then looks up at Nāṣir. "You and your family have done so much for me. I don't know how I can ever repay your kindness."

Nāṣir shakes his head. "You owe us nothing. It is our duty as Shīʿah to do what we can to preserve and spread the teachings of our Imāms (ʿa). You taught us so much all those years in the masjid. Allah granted us this opportunity to serve that same cause."

After several years pass, Khorasan comes alive with rumors of the coming of Imām Riḍā (ʿa). Soon enough, the rumors prove to be true. From his capital in Merv, Maʾmūn, the new Abbasid khalīfah has summoned the Imām (ʿa) to his court. Although he has offered to make the Imām (ʿa) crown prince, his true intentions are revealed when he forces the Imām (ʿa) to accept against his will.

When the Imām (ʿa) enters Khorasan at last, he is greeted by a joyous crowd. Despite the evil of Maʾmūn's schemes, the majority of the people are sincere in their love.
Ibrāhīm is among those who welcome Imām Riḍā (ʿa). He thanks Allah for allowing him to see the Imām (ʿa), though he is upset that he has been brought against his will.

During Imām Riḍā's years in Khorasan, Ibrāhīm devotes his time to acting as his scribe. He records the Imām's every word and does his best to preserve the Imām's wisdom in writing. With the passage of time, Ibrāhīm, already an elderly man when released from prison, becomes older and weaker. However, his love for the Imāms (ʿa) and his passion for learning and teaching the truth is as strong as ever.

One day, Imām Riḍā (ʿa) invites Ibrāhīm to come to his home, which is right next to the masjid. Ibrāhīm respectfully enters the Imām's house. As always, he is prepared to write, with pen and parchment in hand.

"Salāmun ʿalaykum, Ibrāhīm," the Imām (ʿa) says warmly. "I am glad you could come."

"Wa ʿalaykum salām," Ibrāhīm replies. "I am here to serve you in whatever way I can."

"I know you are a faithful scholar and scribe," the Imām (ʿa) says. "I know you have devoted your life to recording and spreading the teachings of the Ahl al-Bayt, and that you have suffered because of your devotion. May Allah reward your efforts! I want to entrust you with one last task." The Imām (ʿa) holds out a tightly scrolled letter for Ibrāhīm to take. "This letter is for my son, Muḥammad, who will be the Imām after me. Will you keep it safe and give it to him after my death?"

Ibrāhīm is speechless for a moment as he reaches out a trembling hand to take the letter. He does not know if he should feel honored to be trusted with such a task, elated at being able to meet the next Imām (ʿa), or grief-stricken to know that Imām Riḍā (ʿa) is already making plans for when he will leave this world.

The Imām (ʿa) sees tears well up in Ibrāhīm's eyes and smiles reassuringly. "Allah has decreed death for all His creatures. If we live an upright life and prepare ourselves for it, death should not be something we fear. Inshāʿ Allāh, we will meet again in the hereafter."

Within a short while, Imām Riḍā (ʿa) is martyred at the hands of Maʾmūn, the son of Hārūn, who killed Imām Kāẓim (ʿa) before him. When Imām Muḥammad al-Jawād (ʿa) comes to bury his father, Ibrāhīm knows it is time to fulfill the promise he had made to the now-martyred Imām.

Imām Jawād (ʿa) is barely eight years of age, yet he carries himself with all the dignity of his fathers and grandfathers before him. Ibrāhīm approaches him and kisses the Imām's hand before gently placing Imām Riḍā's letter in the young Imām's palm.

"Salāmun ʿalaykum, my Imām," Ibrāhīm says. "This is your father's letter to you."

"Wa ʿalaykum salām," replies Imām Jawād (ʿa). He reads the letter and smiles. "Thank you," he whispers. "Thank you—these are truly the words of my beloved father!" He kisses the letter and holds it to his chest. Soon, the letter is wet with tears.

Ibrāhīm moves closer to the Imām (ʿa) and says, "O grandson of Allah's Messenger, you know I would sacrifice my life for you. I can't bear to see you in pain!"

The Imām (ʿa) gives Ibrāhīm a small smile. "Seeing this letter brings me joy," he reassures Ibrāhīm. "My father sends you his final salāms, and he asks Allah to make you his companion in Paradise." He continues, "I also pray to Allah to make you my companion in Paradise."

Ibrāhīm's face shines with light from within, all the more radiant because of his tear-streaked cheeks. "My master—will I truly be your companion in Paradise?" he asks.

Imām Jawād (ʿa) replies, "Yes. By Allah's will, yes, you will."

Ibrāhīm kisses the Imām's hand one last time before they exchange their farewell salāms and he turns to leave. He steps out onto the streets of Khorasan. As he walks home, Ibrāhīm exalts Allah's names and thanks Him for all His blessings.

Once again, a refreshing rain cools the earth, a grove of pomegranate trees draws strength from the life-giving water that soaks into the ground, and the tears on Ibrāhīm's wet cheeks mingle with the small droplets of water falling from the sky above.

CHAPTER 12

Overnight Guest

Aḥmad ibn Muḥammad al-Bazanṭī

A well-dressed young man walks purposefully through the streets of Merv. His name is Aḥmad ibn Muḥammad al-Bazanṭī. He belongs to a noble family that is originally from Mehran, a village near Tehran. He is a companion of Imām Riḍā (ʿa) and is known by the people as a compiler of hundreds of ḥadīth. In keeping with the Prophet's sunnah, he uses a simple, sweet-smelling perfume that brings joy to those around him; and wherever he goes, people love and admire him for his akhlāq. He is always eager to teach those who want to learn and to lend a helping hand to those who need it.

When Aḥmad reaches the marketplace, he ducks into a stall that belongs to a fruit seller. He smiles at the owner and picks out a few pomegranates to buy. As he selects his fruit, he furtively glances around the marketplace, like he is searching for someone. In one far corner, someone else's gaze suddenly meets his own. They nod at each other, and then turn back to buying whatever goods they are buying. A few stalls down, the same thing happens. Aḥmad and another man make eye contact, nod at each other, and then look away. Satisfied, Aḥmad thanks the fruit seller and then continues on his way.

A little ways past the bazaar, he crosses the street and walks up to the front doorstep of a neat and tidy house that sits right next to the masjid. Once again, he quickly and cautiously looks over his shoulder. Once he is sure that the street behind him is quiet, Aḥmad turns back to the door and knocks. Within seconds, the door opens. A servant steps out and graciously gestures Aḥmad into the house. Then,

he, also, looks up and down the street to make sure Aḥmad was not being followed.

Just as Aḥmad and the servant are inside and close the door behind them, there is another knock. They exchange an alarmed glance. The servant signals for Aḥmad to hide in the next room and then slowly opens the door. Peeking out from his hiding place, Aḥmad sees his two friends from the marketplace standing on the front doorstep and sighs with relief.

"Alḥamdulillāh," Aḥmad says once everyone is safely inside. "Salāmun ʿalaykum, Mūsā," he says to the servant. "Thank you. You are very careful when it comes to protecting our master, Imām Riḍā! Muḥammad, Ṣafwān—I'm glad you could both make it as well. I know it is difficult when the Imām is constantly kept under Maʾmūn's watchful eye. We always have to meet with each other under fear of being discovered."

"Let me take you to the Imām," Mūsā says, guiding the three friends into the next room.

The Imām (ʿa) is bent over a letter when they enter his room. When he sees them, he gracefully rises to his feet and welcomes them in. "Salāmun ʿalaykum—Aḥmad, Muḥammad, Ṣafwān. I'm glad you were all able to come. Mūsā—thank you for bringing them safely here. Even in hard times, when our enemy looms over us and breathes down our necks, Allah makes it possible for us to meet with each other."

The three friends reply with a chorus of "wa ʿalaykum salām," and each one takes turns kissing the Imām's hand.

All afternoon, the three friends are engaged in deep conversation with their beloved Imām (ʿa). They ask questions that have been simmering in the back of their minds. They speak about what is troubling them and ask for advice. They seek encouragement, inner strength, and support.

Once evening settles in and the sky begins to darken, Aḥmad, Muḥammad, and Ṣafwān ask permission to leave and return home. The Imām (ʿa) walks his devoted companions to the front door to see them off. Ṣafwān and Muḥammad leave first, each going in opposite directions. As Aḥmad is about to take leave, the Imām (ʿa) gently puts a hand on his shoulder.

"Aḥmad, I'd like you to stay for a while longer," he says.

Puzzled, but tingly with honor and excitement, Aḥmad follows the Imām (ʿa) back into the house. *He must know that I have so many more questions!* he thinks to himself.

Together, they perform wuḍūʾ and pray Maghrib and ʿIshāʾ in the courtyard, under the evening sky. Once it is completely dark, and the night air grows chilly, they sit inside and hold a one-on-one night discussion by candlelight. As a compiler of ḥadīth and teacher of akhlāq, Aḥmad is bursting with questions that he is itching to ask, both for his sake and the sake of his students.

The hours slip away. Aḥmad is completely immersed in conversation with the Imām (ʿa). Before he knows it, it is midnight. Once he runs out of questions, the two of them sit in silence for a few minutes.

The Imām (ʿa) is the first to speak. "Aḥmad, would you like to stay here for the night as my guest?"

For a second, Aḥmad is tongue-tied. Once he is able to speak again, he says, "Whatever you think is best. If you ask me to stay, I will stay. If you ask me to go, I will go." While his tone is humble and respectful, Aḥmad notices himself fighting a funny feeling deep down inside.

"It is better for you to stay here tonight," the Imām (ʿa) says. "There may be soldiers patrolling the streets; it would be uncomfortable to try and explain your situation to them. I don't want to send you into a danger zone."

"Then I'd be honored to spend the night as your guest," Aḥmad says. Again, he feels something that he's never felt before, like a balloon inflating inside his head. The Imām (ʿa) leaves to ask Mūsā to prepare a bed for his guest, and Aḥmad is left alone in the room with a small voice whispering things in his mind.

Out of all my friends, my Imām chose me, he thinks to himself. *He asked me to stay with him and talk. He asked me to stay the night.*

In his mind, Aḥmad tells himself that he has been "chosen" over his friends to spend extra time with the Imām (ʿa) as a special guest. While he is overwhelmed with the honor of being with the Imām (ʿa), instead of feeling grateful and humble, he begins to feel proud. He begins to feel like he is better than his friends.

Aḥmad smiles and takes a deep breath, enjoying the moment. The balloon in his head gets bigger and bigger as his excitement over being the Imām's guest turns into something dangerously close to arrogance.

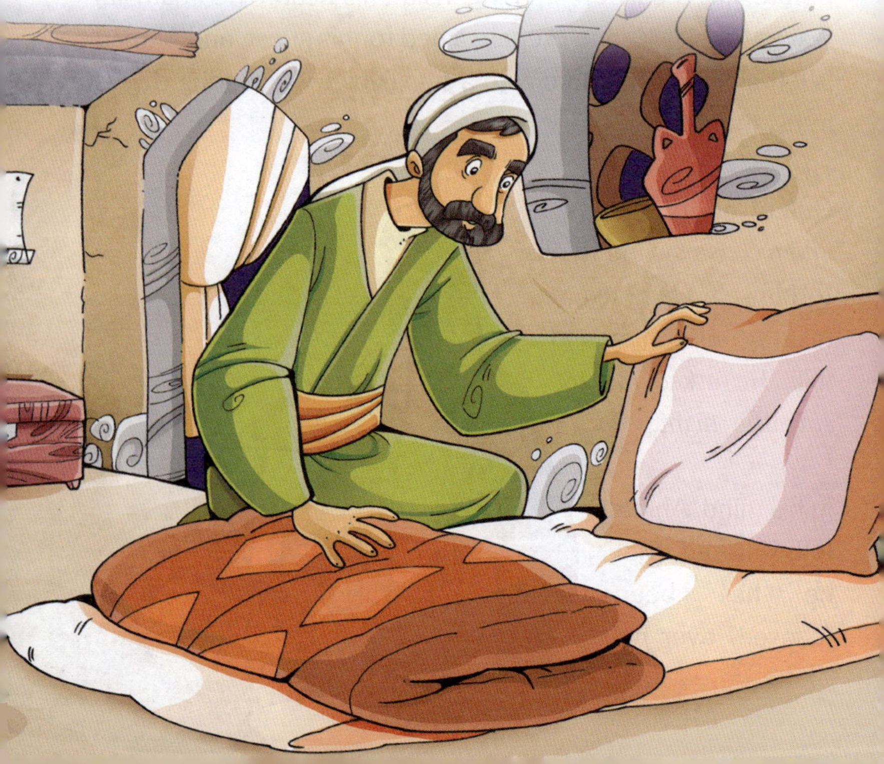

Just then, the Imām (ʿa) reenters the room. "Come, Aḥmad. Your room is ready."

As they walk toward Aḥmad's room, the Imām (ʿa) tells a story:

"My grandfather, the Commander of the Faithful, had a very loyal companion named Ṣaʿṣaʿah. They would visit each other like close friends often do. One time, my grandfather was Ṣaʿṣaʿah's guest for the night. In the morning, when it was time to leave, he turned to Ṣaʿṣaʿah and said, 'I thank Allah for our close friendship, because it is very precious to me. But I ask you not to announce to all your friends that I visited you tonight. You wouldn't want to plant seeds of jealousy among those you love. More importantly, remember we are all servants of Allah. What makes one person better than another is his taqwā and the strength of his connection to Allah, and that is something only He can judge.'"

The Imām (ʿa) concludes his story, and bids Aḥmad a good night. It takes a few minutes for the full meaning of the Imām's words to sink in. Just as he is about to climb into bed, Aḥmad makes the connection between Imām Riḍā's story and his own situation. Imām ʿAlī's words of advice to Ṣaʿṣaʿah echo in his mind, almost as though they are directed toward him: *"Remember we are all servants of Allah. What makes one person better than another is his taqwā and the strength of his connection to Allah, and that is something only He can judge."*

Aḥmad stares into the darkness in wonder and awe. He has always known that the Imāms (ʿa) have access to stores of knowledge granted to them by Allah, but this is the first time he is experiencing this knowledge of the unseen firsthand. Now, he sees that the Imām (ʿa) knew what thoughts had begun to bubble in his mind—

those sneaky beginnings of arrogance—just because he was granted the privilege of staying with the Imām (ʿa) for the night instead of them.

But instead of calling out Aḥmad's mistake and making him feel ashamed, the Imām (ʿa) corrected his mistake so gently, so graciously, so kindly. Aḥmad promises himself that he will learn from the Imām's example and strive to achieve that same level of akhlāq in his interactions with others. He thanks Allah for this opportunity to fix and strengthen his akhlāq. Even though he is a teacher to others, he sees that he, himself, is still a student very much in need of a teacher and guide.

It has been an eventful night. Within a few hours, Aḥmad has learned multiple life lessons.

The Imām (ʿa) reminded him that arrogance takes a person away from Allah, while taqwā and God-consciousness bring believers closer to Allah. As he lies in bed, he prays to Allah that he will never forget these lessons and that he will always be able to put into practice what he has learned. Just before he drifts off to sleep, he hopes he will be able to rise with his host in time to pray Ṣalāt al-Layl and spend some time in worship before dawn.

CHAPTER 13

City of Knowledge

Zakariyyā ibn Ādam

The city of Qom is a center of knowledge and learning. In the eyes of the Abbasid khalīfahs of the time, it isn't very important, and so they pay little attention to it. For them, Qom is nothing special. But for hundreds of scholars and students, Qom is a beautiful city of knowledge and wisdom. It is their home, and it is a place where scholars come together to learn and teach.

The Shīʿah face a lot of persecution in many places throughout the Muslim lands. The corrupt khalīfahs make sure to appoint governors who make life difficult for the Shīʿah. In these difficult times, Qom and other nearby areas in Iran have become safe havens for followers of the Ahl al-Bayt (ʿa). The khalīfahs are too busy with important matters of the state to notice the communities of Shīʿah that have begun to thrive in Iran.

One of the many dedicated scholars that Qom is blessed with is Zakariyyā ibn Ādam. Imām Riḍā (ʿa) loves and respects him very much, and he is in charge of helping and serving the people of Qom on the Imām's behalf. People come to him with their problems, questions, and worries, and he sits down with them to find solutions with the utmost patience and humility. He never makes people feel like they are less than him, or that he is better than them. He never makes them feel like they are ignorant and know nothing. He is kind and gracious in all his interactions. He speaks gently and respectfully to everyone he meets.

While Zakariyyā fulfills his duties as a teacher and scholar in Qom, Imām Riḍā (ʿa) is held in Merv, against his will, in the palace of the Abbasid khalīfah Maʾmūn. Maʾmūn watches his every move very carefully and makes it difficult for the

Imām (ʿa) to meet with his Shīʿah. Through persistence, determination, and love, the people manage to visit their Imām (ʿa) anyway.

After an exhausting journey of 500 miles, one of the Imām's loyal followers arrives in Merv to pay his respects to his master. His name is ʿAlī ibn al-Musayyab, and he has come all the way from Qom. Weariness is written all over his face, and his shoulders are slumped.

The Imām (ʿa) welcomes him warmly, but he notices immediately that something is wrong. Concerned, he asks, "ʿAlī, why do you look so upset? What makes you so unhappy?"

"I am very happy to see you, O grandson of Allah's Messenger!" ʿAlī replies with a sad smile. "But you are right. There is something on my mind. You see, my city, Qom, is very far from here, and it is difficult for me to travel here to Merv. My mind is always churning with questions, but it is impossible for me to bring them to you when you are so far away. What can I do to protect and strengthen my faith against doubt? Who can answer my questions when I can't travel to see you?"

"Don't worry yourself with these thoughts," the Imām (ʿa) replies. "Allah always makes sure that those who are seeking truth will find pathways that lead to guidance. Zakariyyā ibn Ādam is one of my close students; he is someone you can rely on. He has been serving the people of Qom for years, and he will be able to answer many of your questions. If he cannot, then he will bring them to me, and he will help you in whatever way he can."

ʿAlī takes the Imām's hand and kisses it out of gratitude. "Thank you," he says. "You've put my mind at ease."

When he returns home to Qom, he eagerly reaches out to Zakariyyā just as Imām Riḍā (ʿa) recommended, and he is able to benefit from Zakariyyā's scholarship and wisdom like so many other Shīʿah in the same situation.

Before long, Ma'mūn drops his evil charade in Merv and poisons Imām Riḍā ('a). When news of the Imām's death reaches Zakariyyā, he is heartbroken. He remembers all the kindness and the many favors the Imām ('a) had shown him. He remembers the Imām's generous hospitality whenever he would visit Merv. He remembers the long, late-night conversations and question and answer sessions they would have, which would often last until Fajr; then they would perform wuḍū' together and accompany each other to the masjid for Fajr prayers.

Most vividly of all, Zakariyyā remembers the special privilege of being Imām Riḍā's travel companion during Ḥajj one year. That Ḥajj was one of Zakariyyā's most treasured memories. During the entire journey, he was able to bask in the Imām's radiance and benefit from his wisdom. He was even able to visit the graves of the Imām's forefathers in Medina at the side of the Imām ('a) himself.

Imām Riḍā's death has come as a real blow for Zakariyyā. Through a haze of grief and blurred tears, he decides to visit Imām Jawād (ʿa) to offer his condolences.

While Zakariyyā makes the grueling journey from Qom all the way to Baghdad, Imām Jawād (ʿa) sits on his prayer mat with his hands raised and with tears in his eyes. He loves Zakariyyā just as much as his father did, and he never forgets to mention him in his prayers:

"O Allah, please reward Zakariyyā for his loyalty and dedication. He has been a faithful companion, and he has never wavered in serving you. I am happy with him; he has never displeased me or my father, nor has he ever acted against our wishes. So be happy with him, and bless him with abundant blessings in this world and the next."

When Zakariyyā finally arrives at Imām Jawād's doorstep, weary after weeks of travel, the Imām (ʿa) welcomes him with open arms and tends to him with the same generous hospitality his father had been known for. Zakariyyā is not as young as he used to be, and this journey has tired him greatly; but he is refreshed by the presence of the young Imām (ʿa), and he is reminded of the fragrance of his beloved Imām Riḍā (ʿa).

After his visit with Imām Jawād (ʿa), Zakariyyā returns to Qom. As the years pass, he continues to serve the people of Qom with passion and vigor despite his aging, weakening body. Wisdom is written in every line of his face, and the people come to seek his advice and take with them a ray of that wisdom.

Hundreds of miles away, Imām Jawād (ʿa) stands on his prayer mat, bowed in rukūʿ, when one of his servants enters the room. Respectfully, he waits for the Imām (ʿa) to finish his prayer. The Imām (ʿa) ends his prayer, and then looks up. "What has happened, ʿAmmār?" he asks.

There is a short pause before ʿAmmār speaks. He lowers his gaze, and there is sadness in his eyes. "My master—your old friend and companion, Zakariyyā ibn Ādam... he has passed away."

The Imām (ʿa) lets out a soft sigh. He is still young, but the responsibility on his shoulders is great. His sigh could easily have been that of a much older, more experienced man.

"We belong to Allah, and to Him we shall return,[1]" he says after a moment of silence. "Peace be to him the day he was

1 Noble Qurʾān, 2:156

born, the day he dies, and the day he will be raised alive.[2]" The Imām (ʿa) quotes the words Allah uses in Sūrah Maryam in praise of Prophet Yaḥyā (ʿa), the same words Prophet ʿĪsā (ʿa) used to describe himself.

"He was always truthful when he spoke and patient in the face of trials," Imām Jawād (ʿa) continues, remembering the life of his faithful companion. "He always did what would please Allah, and so he earned the love of Allah and His Prophet (ṣ). He was a pure and sincere soul. May Allah bless him."

2 Noble Qur'ān, 19:15

Back in Qom, the streets are packed with mourners at Zakariyyā's funeral. Imām Ṣādiq (ʿa) once said, "When a believing scholar dies, a gaping hole is made in the fortress of Islam, which nothing can patch."[3] In the case of Zakariyyā, no one will feel this loss more than the people of Qom.

The funeral procession follows the bearers of Zakariyyā's body to what will come to be known as the Graveyard of the Shaykhayn, next to the future ḥaram of Sayyidah Maʿṣūmah, where he is finally laid to rest.

3 Al-Kāfī 2.7.2

CHAPTER 14

The Imām's Defender

Abū aṣ-Ṣalt (ʿAbd as-Salām ibn Ṣāliḥ al-Harawī)

The streets of Nishapur are packed so tightly that the enormous caravan can barely squeeze through. A man with a noble face rides a camel near the front, and people call out to him, hoping to be heard along with hundreds of other voices that fill the air.

"Salāmun ʿalaykum, O grandson of the Messenger of Allah!"

"Master, I am at your service!"

"Accept my salāms, my beloved Imām Riḍā!"

Abū aṣ-Ṣalt weaves his way through the thick crowds until he gets a clear view of the Imām (ʿa). It has been a long time since they last were together in Medina. He smiles, remembering the days he would spend at the Imām's side—watching, learning, serving. He remembers how he would jot down every bit of wisdom the Imām (ʿa) shared and how he would leap to his feet to perform the simplest tasks for the Imām's sake. As he watches Imām Riḍā (ʿa) ride down the street toward where he stands, Abū aṣ-Ṣalt wishes with all his heart that those days would come again.

He gazes hopefully at the Imām (ʿa), trying to make eye contact. In a voice barely above a whisper, he asks, "Master, can I come with you?" His words are immediately drowned out by hundreds of other voices, but, still, he mouths the words, "Master, let me come with you!"

Just as the the Imām (ʿa) passes where Abū aṣ-Ṣalt stands, he turns his head toward his loyal companion and gives a slight nod, as if to say, "I would love your company, my old friend."

Nothing is as it seems, Abū aṣ-Ṣalt thinks to himself as he joins the Imām's caravan on its way to Merv, the capital of the Abbasid khalīfah Maʾmūn. From the outside, it looks like Maʾmūn has invited Imām Riḍā (ʿa) to his palace, offering him a position of great honor. In reality, however, he orders his men to take the longest, most difficult, most dangerous route. As a result, a journey that could have taken two months ends up taking more than a year.

But no matter how hard he tries, Ma'mūn cannot extinguish the love that people have for the Imām (ʿa). As his caravan passes from city to city, lovers of the Ahl al-Bayt (ʿa) crowd the streets to welcome him. They do not realize that his every step takes him closer and closer to deadly danger.

But Abū aṣ-Ṣalt does. Nothing is as it seems. The Imām (ʿa) is oddly quiet. While he responds graciously to the warm welcome he receives from the people, Abū aṣ-Ṣalt can sense that this is not what he wanted. Behind this grand and glorious show, Ma'mūn is hatching a wicked plot, and Abū aṣ-Ṣalt knows it.

As they near Merv, more and more soldiers join the caravan. They make Abū aṣ-Ṣalt feel like he is trapped with Imām Riḍā (ʿa) in a moving prison. He isn't able to talk as much as he would like with his Imām since they are never given any privacy, but he has been able to piece together most of Ma'mūn's sly, slippery plan.

The truth is that Ma'mūn isn't as strong and powerful as he wants to be. The Abbasid empire is split between Ma'mūn and his brother, Amīn. Ma'mūn wants to build a strong base of supporters so he can defeat Amīn. He hopes that by making it look like Imām Riḍā (ʿa) is on his side, he will gain the support of all the lovers of the Ahl al-Bayt (ʿa) who live throughout his territory. Then he will be strong enough to win control of the entire Abbasid empire.

But that isn't all. For a long time, the Imāms have been an especially dangerous threat to Abbasid rule because they are the Prophet's rightful successors. If Maʾmūn announces that Imām Riḍā (ʿa) is his successor, he might be able to silence those who have been demanding for years that the right to rule be returned to the Ahl al-Bayt (ʿa).

Abū aṣ-Ṣalt sighs. He knows that Maʾmūn's schemes will have far-reaching consequences. Politics can quickly

become a messy, dirty business. By dragging the Imām (ʿa) into his political ambitions, Maʾmūn will be able to keep a close eye on him and plant seeds of doubt in the minds of the Shīʿah. Abū aṣ-Ṣalt worries that they will begin to think that their Imām (ʿa) is interested in material power because of Maʾmūn's treacherous offer.

It is up to those who can see through a plot to reveal the trickery behind it, so Abū aṣ-Ṣalt promises himself that he will not let Maʾmūn mislead the people and turn them against the Imām (ʿa). Merv is already full of enemies. Abū aṣ-Ṣalt prays to Allah that he will be able to protect his Imām and create awareness among the Shīʿah so that he will not have to face enemies that once used to be his friends.

Abū aṣ-Ṣalt's suspicions quickly prove to be true. Maʾmūn makes a great show of appointing Imām Riḍā (ʿa) as crown prince and successor to the throne. He orders new coins to be minted with both his name and the Imām's name engraved on them. He even decrees that the black cloth traditionally used by the Abbasids for banners and flags should be replaced with green cloth, the color of the Ahl al-Bayt (ʿa).

At the same time, he treats the Imām (ʿa) like a prisoner. He always has him followed, "escorted" by soldiers wherever he goes. It hurts Abū aṣ-Ṣalt to see his Imām trapped in enemy territory. Even worse, although he can see the reality of the situation—that the Imām (ʿa) is being held against his will—not everyone does.

The reactions of the people are mixed. Some celebrate the fact that Imām Riḍā (ʿa) is now crown prince. They are excited that the divinely guided Imāms from the Ahl al-Bayt (ʿa) are going to be restored as rightful leaders of the Muslim ummah. They don't realize that Maʾmūn has no intention of handing his power over to the Imām (ʿa), and that he only wants to get more power for himself. They don't realize that once Maʾmūn has his empire under control, he will no longer have any need for the Imām (ʿa). They don't know that the Imām (ʿa) himself told Maʾmūn, "I will accept this position because I have no choice, but it means nothing because I will leave this world before you."

Other people are angry and confused. They know that Maʾmūn is evil and cannot be trusted, and they are shocked that Imām Riḍā (ʿa) has accepted a position in such a corrupt government. They don't realize that he only accepted because Maʾmūn threatened to kill him otherwise. Their anger toward the Imām (ʿa), because of their misunderstanding, is what hurts Abū aṣ-Ṣalt the most.

He hears the same disbelieving whisper repeated over and over again: "Why would the Imām accept such an offer?" He hears the Imām's own Shīʿah asking each other, "Why would he betray us and everything he taught us to stand for?"

The rumors only get worse, especially since Maʾmūn is behind them. He recruits his hypocrite friends and tells them to keep on feeding lies to the public:

"Maʾmūn and the Imām are obviously good friends. Why else would they be working together?"

"It's clear that the Imām wanted more power. This was his plan all along!"

"The Imām is no different from the Abbasid king. They are both selfish and hungry for power. What's the point in following him anymore?"

To Abū aṣ-Ṣalt, each of these accusations feels like a stab in the back. This is what he'd feared the most: when friends turn into enemies because of lies and deceit. He reminds himself of his promise to defend the Imām (ʿa) and to undo whatever damage Maʾmūn might try to inflict on the Shīʿah of the Ahl al-Bayt (ʿa).

When Imām Riḍā (ʿa) goes out in public, Abū aṣ-Ṣalt insists on accompanying him.

"Master, I'm coming with you!" he says. "We don't know anymore who is still a friend and who has been poisoned by Maʾmūn's lies. I'm afraid you'll be in danger no matter where you go. Let me come with you and protect you." Out of habit, he looks over his shoulder to make sure there are no guards prowling around. Then, he lowers his voice and says, "I don't trust anything that tyrant says about trying to keep you safe."

They are passing through the marketplace when an ignorant, fiery young man shouts at the Imām (ʿa), "Why did you abandon your followers and join those who have always oppressed us?" Abū aṣ-Ṣalt seizes the opportunity to open this young man's eyes to the truth. He turns to face him and speaks passionately, but softly. He has just noticed two guards lurking in the shadow of a fruit stand, and he doesn't want to cause any trouble for the Imām (ʿa), who is standing right next to him.

"Do you think that the Imām wanted any of this to happen?" he demands. He hopes that his harsh tone will bring the man to his senses and make him more ready to listen. "Do you think he wanted to be snatched from his family in Medina and brought all the way here, hundreds of miles away from home? Would you rather have had your Imām killed at the hands of impatient soldiers in Medina, or would you rather have him here, in Merv, alive? I promise you that he did not come here by choice, but by force. If he had refused, he would have been killed. It would only have resulted in more violence against the Ahl al-Bayt (ʿa) and their Shīʿah. The Imām did not betray you. He is protecting you and looking out for you, just as he always has."

The young man is speechless for a moment. He takes a step closer to the Imām (ʿa), his knees trembling. Abū aṣ-Ṣalt watches him carefully. "Master, forgive me," he stammers. "I

was... so confused and... so angry. I didn't really stop to think. I'm very sorry." He glances shamefaced at Abū aṣ-Ṣalt. "What can I do to make up for what I've done?"

"Tell people the truth," Abū aṣ-Ṣalt says, speaking more gently this time. "Lots of other people are confused as well, and that's why they are angry. Maʾmūn wants to deceive you into thinking that the Imām is interested in wealth and status. He wants to make you lose faith. Don't let him win. Help us fight back against these oppressors."

"How can we fight back?" the man whispers, looking back and forth between Abū aṣ-Ṣalt and the Imām (ʿa), who has listened quietly until now. "What can we do?"

"We must trust in Allah," the Imām (ʿa) says, speaking for the first time, "and do what we can. We must stay alert and be aware of the reality of our situation. Abū aṣ-Ṣalt is right. Tell people the truth. Help clear their minds of this disease Maʾmūn has tried so hard to spread. I will also do whatever I can to undo Maʾmūn's

work from within. I will not play his game, at least not by his rules. I will take no part in his oppression. Instead, I will use every opportunity to continue performing my duties as your Imām, your leader, and your guide."

"Thank you, my Imam," the man says. "I will do everything I can to spread the word. I am and always will be at your service." With a quiet "was salām," he slips away, leaving Abū aṣ-Ṣalt with Imām Riḍā (ʿa). The two soldiers were too busy arguing with the fruit-seller to notice that anything had happened at all.

Slowly, but surely, Abū aṣ-Ṣalt works to reveal Maʾmūn's treachery to the Shīʿah and put their hearts and minds at ease. In the severe circumstances that he and the Imām (ʿa) are in, there is only so much that he can do. But he makes the most of the situation and takes advantage of every opportunity to speak with people—whether in private, in the marketplace, or on the side of the street—making sure he is not noticed by Maʾmūn's soldiers. He shows them how foolish it is to trust the words of their enemies over their Imām (ʿa) and urges them to think carefully before believing what they hear.

"Don't jump to conclusions," he advises them. "Don't blindly accept rumors as true. You need to make sure you have enough information—enough proof—before you make a final judgement. Our enemies will try to confuse us with lies and false claims, so we shouldn't believe anything they say until we see solid proof."

He is very patient as he helps people understand what a dirty game politics can become when greedy rulers don't play fair, and he warns them that a clever, evil person can make lies look like truth and truth look like lies.

However, even though he is grateful and relieved that the Shīʿah have renewed faith in their Imām (ʿa), Abū aṣ-Ṣalt still feels uneasy. As long as Imām Riḍā (ʿa) is near Maʾmūn, he is not safe, and Abū aṣ-Ṣalt is deathly afraid that there will come a time when he will not be able to protect him.

Summer days in Merv are warm and sunny, but nights are usually much cooler. One evening, the earth decides not to let go of its daytime heat. Long after the sun sets, the air is thick and hot, and Abū aṣ-Ṣalt finds it difficult to breathe.

He paces back and forth in the Imām Riḍā's private chambers, which are adjacent to the masjid, alone. He had been visiting the Imām (ʿa) that afternoon when Maʾmūn summoned his newly-appointed crown prince for some sort of special meeting. With a sinking feeling in his heart, Abū aṣ-Ṣalt watched the two soldiers lead the Imām (ʿa) out of the room. That happened hours ago, and it's already past Maghrib time, but the Imām (ʿa) still hasn't returned. The sinking feeling has only gotten worse.

Sick with worry, Abū aṣ-Ṣalt stops pacing and looks around the room, hoping to find something that will give him some relief. He spots a copy of the Qurʾān lying on a small table. Just the sight of the Qurʾān makes Abū aṣ-Ṣalt feel a little bit better. It reminds him of the infinite wisdom of Allah, who knows every person's deepest fears and is the source of all comfort.

He picks up the Qurʾan and feels its cover, worn down by the Imām's touch over the years, and carefully opens it. One verse on the page stands out to him from all the rest: "Surely we are from Allah, and to Him we shall return."[1] The words comfort him, but as

1 *Noble Qurʿān, 2:156*

he reads them, he feels a twinge of sadness. Just then, the door creaks open, and the Imām (ʿa) enters the room.

Abū aṣ-Ṣalt leaps to his feet. "Master!" he exclaims. "I was beginning to worry! Is everything—" he stops short. The room is dark, so he couldn't see the Imām (ʿa) properly at first. As he steps closer, he sees that the Imām (ʿa) is in pain. His body is trembling violently, and his legs don't seem to be able to carry his weight. Just as the Imām's knees are about to give way, Abū aṣ-Ṣalt grabs his arm to steady him before he falls. "Put your arm around my neck," he manages to say, breathing heavily. "Lean on me. Let me take you to your bed."

Abū aṣ-Ṣalt is not a young man, and he staggers as he strains to support the Imām (ʿa). But he uses every last ounce of his strength to safely lay him in bed. The Imām's forehead is feverish, and he is shivering. Abū aṣ-Ṣalt covers him lightly with a sheet. Then he sinks to his knees by the bedside, his face wet with tears.

"He poisoned you." It isn't a question. "That

twisted Maʾmūn poisoned you!" He takes the Imām's hand and presses it to his forehead. "We both knew this would happen," he says, choked with tears. "I just didn't know when."

"You've been true and faithful until the end," the Imām (ʿa) says. Every word is a struggle; every breath is a struggle. "I've taught you what you need to do. I've prepared my Shīʿah for this moment as well as I could. I am ready to meet my Lord." He says nothing for a moment just so he can breathe. Then he speaks in a soft, strained whisper. "My son, Muḥammad, will be here soon. Will you go outside to see if he has arrived? I need to speak with him... one last time."

A question forces its way through a haze of grief to Abū aṣ-Ṣalt's lips. "Master—how is this possible? Your son is in Medina, and we are in Merv, hundreds of miles away!"

The Imām (ʿa) almost smiles. "Allah makes it possible. Go outside and show him the way in; he is here." Before Abū aṣ-Ṣalt leaves the room, the Imām (ʿa) gives his final instructions for when his son comes. "Leave us alone for a few minutes, and let us talk in private. When we are finished, you may enter. If you see that my eyes are closed and my cloak covers my chest, know that I am resting. If you see that my son has pulled my cloak over my head, know that I have left this world as a shahīd."

The young boy's face seems to shine with a soft light as Abū aṣ-Ṣalt leads him to his father's room. Before opening the door, Abū aṣ-Ṣalt kneels before the child—only then are they the same height—and looks into his eyes. "After your father, you are my Imām. I promise to do my best to protect you as long as Allah permits. Please know that you have my love and my loyalty forever." He kisses the boy's forehead, then his hand, and stands up. "Your father is waiting." He watches the young Muḥammad al-Jawād (ʿa) push the big door open and thinks to himself, So young, yet so dignified. So innocent, yet so wise. After meeting Imām Riḍā's successor, Abū aṣ-Ṣalt realizes that age means nothing when Allah chooses someone as a divine leader and guide.

Abū aṣ-Ṣalt waits obediently outside Imām Riḍā's room, though his heart whispers to him that he should not leave his Imām (ʿa) alone. But he is not alone. He is with his son. They are together, he tells himself. For a while, he is lost in his thoughts, until he sees a small figure standing before him, in front of the open door. It is Imām Jawād (ʿa). Abū aṣ-Ṣalt searches his young face for a hint, a glimmer—any trace of a tear—but it is difficult to see in the dark. There is nothing to do except enter the room and see the truth for himself.

The window is open now, and the room is faintly lit by the moon. In the bed, against the wall, lies a still figure draped in a sheet and covered with a cloak. By the light of the moon, Abū aṣ-Ṣalt can see that the cloak covers not just the body of his beloved master, but it is pulled over his head as well.

He can no longer hold back his tears, so he doesn't try. He sits down under the open window, puts his head in his hands, and weeps. He feels someone sit down next to him, and he knows that he is not alone in his pain. The young Imām Jawād (ʿa) is there with him, and they mourn their loss together, sharing each other's grief. They both carry a great, aching emptiness in their hearts. It is an emptiness that can only be filled by following in the footsteps of the one they lost and keeping his legacy alive.

The world will never be without a divine leader. Even as Imām Jawād (ʿa) mourns his father's death, he is ready to shoulder the responsibilities that come with being the next Imam.

CHAPTER 15

Searching for Light

Ḥasan ibn Saʿīd

Chapter 15

It is a warm summer day in Ahvaz. Ḥasan ibn Saʿīd walks briskly to the masjid. He always makes an extra effort to be on time for prayer, but he still makes sure to return people's greetings and smile at the familiar faces he passes on the way.

Ḥasan's family has a long history of serving the Ahl al-Bayt (ʿa). His ancestors were all among the companions of the Maʿṣūmīn (ʿa). His grandfather, Ḥumād ibn Mihrān, had been a student of Imām Sajjād (ʿa) for many years in Medina. Now, all these generations later, Ḥasan and his brother Ḥusayn continue their family's legacy by devoting themselves to the Imām of their time, Imām Muḥammad al-Jawād (ʿa).

The two brothers have travelled to many places together in search of knowledge, sometimes seeking it from the ultimate source, Imām Jawād (ʿa) himself. Both are scholars and compilers of thousands of ḥadīth, with dozens of books to their names. Despite all their achievements, they never feel satisfied with what they have done; they continue on their path of learning

with just as much passion and humility as when they first started.

As he nears the masjid, Ḥasan thinks fondly of his brother. The book of ḥadith he holds in his hands brings back lots of memories of the journeys they would go on together in search of knowledge and wisdom. He has learned almost everything that he knows with Ḥusayn at his side; now, he wishes that they could teach what they've learned together as well. Ḥasan usually gives a short sermon after prayers at the masjid and shares some ḥadīth from one of his collections. Sometimes he ends up using Ḥusayn's notes, and wishes Ḥusayn were here to share the nuggets of wisdom that he had so carefully gathered.

The masjid is teeming with people coming in from the busy streets. By the time the adhān begins, everyone is arranged in nice, neat rows. After prayer, Ḥasan sits on the minbar and opens his book of ḥadīth. As he

recites the ones he selected for today and explains their meaning, his mind takes him to the places where he learned each ḥadīth. If he learned it directly from the Imām (ʿa), he replays the Imām's explanation in his head and tries his best to communicate the same message with all its depth and beauty.

Everyone in the masjid is all ears. For a few minutes, they put the busy, dusty streets behind them and take time to nourish their souls.

Once the sermon is finished, the masjid empties as people file out and return to their shops and stalls or whatever work they were doing before.

Ḥasan is one of the last to leave. He

emerges into the bright sunlight, thinking of the one face he hadn't seen in the masjid—his friend ʿAbdullāh. This isn't much of a surprise; ʿAbdullāh hardly ever comes to the masjid. But Ḥasan still nurses a secret hope that one day, he will see ʿAbdullāh in the congregation, listening. Since it is clear he won't find ʿAbdullāh here, Ḥasan decides to go to his friend's candle shop in the bazaar.

"Salāmun ʿalaykum, ʿAbdullāh!" Ḥasan says cheerfully. "I missed you at the masjid."

ʿAbdullāh gives Ḥasan a smile, half playful, half mocking. "Wa ʿalaykum salām. Tell me, what wise words did you recite for people today?"

Ḥasan returns the smile, unfazed by the slight sarcasm in ʿAbdullāh's tone. "Why don't you come to the masjid yourself and see?"

"I don't have time for that," ʿAbdullāh replies shortly, looking down at the wax he is pouring into a candle mold.

Ḥasan quickly changes the subject, realizing that ʿAbdullāh isn't in the mood for lectures and speeches. "What are you working on?" he asks.

But underneath the casual question, Ḥasan is worried about his friend. If only there was a way to open his eyes to the light around him and the wonderful treasures within his reach: the wise teachings of the Imāms, the spiritual community at the masjid, and the blessings and mercy of Allah who is always ready to give to those who ask.

After talking for a few minutes about how business has been lately for ʿAbdullāh's shop, Ḥasan tells ʿAbdullāh that he needs to get going. They exchange salāms, and ʿAbdullāh watches Ḥasan walk away, feeling strangely empty and sad inside.

At Maghrib time one evening, for the first time in a long time, Ḥasan is running late for prayer. The streets are almost empty. Most people have already closed up their shops and are making their way to the masjid.

As he is passing by the bazaar, Ḥasan suddenly hears a familiar voice cry for help. He turns around and sees ʿAbdullāh's candle shop wreathed in an orange flicker. It is on fire.

Ḥasan sprints toward the growing blaze to help his friend.

"'Abdullāh! 'Abdullāh! Are you alright?"
"Ḥasan! Please—get help! Get more water!" 'Abdullāh shouts as he douses the flames with a bucket of water. "We need to stop the fire before it spreads to the candles and the wax! Then water won't do any good."

Ḥasan grabs a bucket and races to the nearest well. So far only the outer walls of the stall are on fire. But if the wax catches fire... Ḥasan shudders to think of the consequences.

Thankfully, after Ḥasan and 'Abdullāh make a couple of trips to the well, they are able to extinguish the fire. 'Abdullāh looks forlornly at the wet, smoky ruins of his shop.

"I don't know how to thank you enough," he says to Ḥasan. "It could've been so much worse. Now I've made you delay your prayers, and I know you always like to be on time. How can I ever repay you?"

"Alḥamdulillāh, by Allah's grace, we avoided the worst," Ḥasan says. "And there is nothing to repay—it was the least I could do. Besides, Imām Riḍā (ʿa) has taught us not to expect reward from people when we do an act for Allah. If we sincerely perform a good deed for Allah's pleasure, then, inshāʾAllāh, our reward will be with Him. We don't do good deeds in exchange for gifts, favors, or praise. We strive to do them purely for His sake."

ʿAbdullāh is silent for a moment. *I wouldn't mind hearing more of that*, he thinks to himself. Those are powerful words. Then, to Ḥasan, he says, "Thank you so much anyway. I don't want to keep you any longer; it's getting late."

"Let me know if you need any help cleaning up," Ḥasan offers. "I can come in the morning when we have more light to see by." They exchange salāms, and Ḥasan sets off for home, eager to pray. Tonight, his home will be his masjid.

The next day, after Ẓuhr and ʿAṣr prayers, when Ḥasan turns and addresses the gathering, he sees ʿAbdullāh's face beaming at him from a row in the back. He smiles as he begins his sermon with Allah's name.

After his speech, Ḥasan hurries through the crowd, hoping to catch ʿAbdullāh before he leaves the masjid.
"Salāmun ʿalaykum, ʿAbdullāh!" he calls out when he spots him. "You came!"

ʿAbdullāh turns to face Ḥasan and smiles. "I saw the wisdom

in the words you shared last night. Even in all the chaos of putting out the fire, your actions reflected the teachings of the Imāms. You showed me, through your actions, that they've given us guidance about everything in life. I realized that they are truly looking out for us and have our best interests at heart, and that I would only be hurting myself if I ignore what they have to share."

"Those were the Imām's words, not mine," Ḥasan says, humbly. "You can't imagine how happy I am that you saw the beauty in them."

"Alḥamdulillāh," ʿAbdullāh says at last. "Allah has helped me find the light I've been missing for so long."

CHAPTER 16

The Poor Man's Treasure

ʿAlī ibn Mahziyār al-Ahwāzī

"Father, I'm hungry," little Muḥammad says to his father, ʿAlī. They've just finished their meager meal of coarse barley bread. Muḥammad, his sister, his brother, his mother, and his father each only ate a few bites before the hunk of bread was finished, and their stomachs are far from full.

"I know you are," ʿAlī says, a pained look on his face. "I am, too. But let's still thank Allah for what we have now, and, inshāʿAllāh, He will give us more. He is always very generous, and He has told us in the Qur'ān: If you are thankful, I will give you more.[1]"

Little Muḥammad nods, but he can feel his stomach rumbling, asking for more now.

"Here," his mother says gently, handing him a bowl of water. "Drink some. It'll help fill you up."

1 Noble Qur'ān, 14:7

Late that night, ʿAlī is deep in prayer. His forehead presses against his turbah as he whispers to Allah in sajdah.

"O Allah! Send your blessings on the Prophet (ṣ) and his family. Help his successors as they guide and lead the Muslim ummah, and protect them from their enemies. Help us, as Shīʿah, to stay strong and to remain loyal to our Imāms, especially to the Imām of our time, Imām Jawād (ʿa)."

He is silent for a few moments before continuing. "O Allah! You know best what my needs are, and I know that You are the only one who can fulfill my needs. I am a poor man. Not a day goes by when my family isn't hungry. Sometimes I feel like I'm not taking care of them properly, and that I'm failing them in some way. Allah, You provide sustenance to all Your creatures. You give to whomever You wish, and You give according to Your wisdom. If You have decided that it is better for me and my family to remain poor, then I am content. But if You have not, then, for the sake of my wife and children, help

me earn enough to feed and clothe them properly. Whatever Your decision may be, help us to be happy and content with what we have, and to turn to You whenever we are in need. And let us never forget the precious treasures that we do have, because being rich means more than just having money."

After a long time, he finally raises his head. There is a round bump on his forehead where it touched the turbah, a souvenir of the many hours he has spent with it pressed against hardened clay out of humility before his Lord.

The next day, ʿAlī steps out of his home, ready to do his best to bring home something to eat for his family. After working as a teacher for many years, despite his poverty, ʿAlī has earned the deepest respect of the people of Ahvaz. In fact, people can hardly tell that he is poor just from looking at him. He carries himself with quiet dignity, and while his clothes are simple, they are neat and clean.

He heads in the direction of one of his young students who is learning to read Qur'ān, his first student of the day. As he patiently reviews the letters and how to connect the sounds to form words, he weaves other lessons into his Qur'ān lessons, teaching the little boy bits of wisdom he has learned from the Imāms. When he finishes the lesson, he talks with the parents, listening to any questions they might have, and he promises that he will ask Imām Jawād (ʿa) the next time he is able to send a letter. The boy's father hands ʿAlī a small pouch of coins to show his gratitude. ʿAlī thanks him, and continues on his way.

Late that afternoon, on his way home, ʿAlī stops at the marketplace to buy some food for his family's dinner. He chooses a couple of loaves of barley bread, and then pauses. With a pang, he remembers little Muḥammad's small voice saying "Father, I'm hungry," and the worried, tired look on his wife's face. A few stalls down, he sees a vendor selling dates and pomegranates. After buying the bread, he peers into his pouch of coins. There are still a few left. He hurries over to the fruit stand, asks for a bunch of dates and two pomegranates, and hands over the last of his coins. Then he heads for home with a spring in his step, his heart much lighter than before.

"Alḥamdulillāh," he whispers gratefully.

When ʿAlī comes home, his children rush to greet him and shower him with hugs and kisses. Muḥammad brings him some water while his siblings help their mother lay out the food for their meal. The children's eyes grow wide when they see the sweet, succulent dates. Their mother's eyes light up when she sees the two round, ruby red pomegranates, bursting with juice.

"Oh, ʿAlī—what a treat!" she exclaims finally.

ʿAlī beams at her. "I got them especially for you," he says. "And the dates are all for you three," he says, smiling at Muḥammad and his siblings.

"Alḥamdulillah," his wife says, and the children echo her thanks.

This time, they all finish their meal, satisfied, and they thank Allah, just as they always do—whether their bellies are full or not.

One evening, after his children go to bed on mostly empty stomachs, ʿAlī stays awake, reading a letter he has just finished writing by candlelight. It is a letter for Imām Jawād (ʿa), full of the questions ʿAlī has been asked by the people of his city. In the letter, ʿAlī also asks for instructions on what he can do that will help the Imām (ʿa) the most. Tomorrow, inshāʿAllāh, he will send the letter with a caravan heading from Ahvaz to Baghdad, and then he will simply have to wait for a reply. It could be a few months before the caravan returns.

ʿAlī sighs. He knows he must be patient, but it is difficult to be so far from the Imām (ʿa). It is also difficult to fight enemies he cannot see. At this point, ignorance, lies, and misunderstanding are some of the biggest enemies the Shīʿah face, and ʿAlī does whatever he can to battle falsehood with the truth by teaching and educating those around him.

After a few minutes lost in thought, ʿAlī blows out the candle and lies down on the thin mattress that is his bed. Soon, he drifts off to sleep.

In the morning, after Fajr, ʿAlī waits for the sun to rise, bent in sajdah. As the first rays of the sun shine through the window, he looks tenderly at his sleeping wife and children.

"O Allah!" he prays, "Help me be a good servant to you and a good husband and father to them!"

At long last, Imām Jawād's reply comes with a small trading caravan. ʿAlī hurries home, eager to open it and read what the Imām (ʿa) has to say. He shows it to his wife, and, together, they read:

In the name of Allah, the All-Beneficent, the All-Merciful

Salāmun ʿalaykum dearest ʿAlī,

May Allah fill your life in this world with blessing and admit you in the next world to Paradise. I pray that He rewards you for your efforts in this world and the hereafter and that he gathers you with His special friends on the Day of Judgment.

I know Allah has challenged you through many tests to see the true strength of your faith, and you have passed every single one of those tests. Your patience in the face of hardship, your dedication to the cause of the Ahl al-Bayt, your concern for the well-being of your family—don't think that any of it has gone unnoticed. Allah knows and rewards every good deed, even if it is the size of a mustard seed.[2]

I hope it comforts you to know that you have treasures that are worth more than all the wealth in the world combined. On the Day of Judgment, your face will be radiant with joy, and others will wish that they could give up all the wealth they ever had in exchange for what you have: strong faith and Allah's pleasure.

I am very grateful for all the work you are doing. Your loyalty and devotion means more to me than a mountain of gold or silver. If there is anything you need, all you have to do is ask. There will always be someone there to listen.

Was salām

ʿAlī hugs the letter to his chest, tears of joy trickling from the corners of his eyes, and then he hugs his wife.

"Alḥamdulillāh," she says. "We are blessed to have such a precious treasure buried deep inside our hearts: love for the Ahl al-Bayt and our Imāms."

2 Noble Qur'ān, 21:47

ʿAlī smiles. "You're right. Whenever I receive a letter from our Imām, I forget that I am poor. I feel like the richest man in the world."

That night, ʿAlī decides to stay up and worship until dawn out of gratitude to Allah. He goes into sajdah, and all his needs, worries, and requests tumble out of his mouth in a whispered prayer.

"O Allah! Help me continue to serve the Imām in the best possible way. Help him guide people to the path of Your pleasure. Help people to see past the lies that Your enemies disguise as the truth."

He remembers the last lines of the Imām's letter: If there is anything you need, all you have to do is ask. There will always be someone there to listen.

He continues, "O Allah, You have blessed me with riches worth far more than gold and silver; I only ask You for enough worldly wealth to feed my family so that we can better fulfill our duties toward You and our Imām."

Then, ʿAlī sits up and stares into the room's soft darkness, thinking. He knows that Allah's way of answering duʿā is a beautiful, complex, intricate process. He knows that Allah hears whenever His servants call on Him. He knows that Allah accepts every sincere prayer. But he also knows that Allah decides on the best way to answer a prayer, and it may not happen the way His servants expect it to happen. He might delay His response as a test, or because He wants to give His servants the reward of extra prayers by waiting for them to repeat their requests. He might decide something else is a better choice.

Or He might want His servants to realize the status of His special friends and use them to get closer to Him.

That must be it! ʿAlī thinks to himself. Perhaps he can ask Allah through Imām Jawād (ʿa). If his sins are acting as a barrier between him and his Lord, the Imām (ʿa) is free of any such barrier. Surely the Imām's prayer will work as a ladder that his own prayer can climb to reach Allah. There are many ways to make a duʿā, but one of the best ways is for that duʿā to begin its journey to Allah from the lips of an Imām. Allah Himself has designed duʿā this way.

In the next letter he sends, ʿAlī includes a small note at the end:

Please keep my family in your prayers. You know our situation. I am content with what I already have, but it is hard to watch my children go to bed hungry each night. If Allah decides to increase my worldly sustenance, I pray I do not forget what kind of blessing is the greater treasure.

Months later comes the Imām's reply:

Dearest 'Alī,

May Allah reward you for everything you have sacrificed for His sake. I pray that He grants you and your family the best of things in this world and the next, and that your every need is fulfilled. But know that your dedication to Islam is greater than any wealth.

Was salām

Tingling with joy from head to toe, 'Alī knows that the Imām ('a) is right. Faith is a treasure that money cannot buy. A poor man with faith will be much better off than a rich man with no faith on Judgment Day, when worldly wealth will mean nothing.

ʿAlī promises himself that he will not let money distract him from seeking Allah's pleasure, a treasure that even the poorest of men can afford.

Epilogue

As a result of the Imam's prayer, Allah bestows abundant worldly blessings on ʿAlī's family. Even so, they never forget what has true value. After Imām Jawād's martyrdom, ʿAlī continues to be a loyal follower of Imām Hādī (ʿa). He works tirelessly to serve the Imāms, support the Shīʿah, and fight the Imāms' enemies. He writes dozens of books and narrates hundreds of ḥadīth, battling lies with the truth, and preserving the teachings of the Ahl al-Bayt (ʿa).

Near the end of his life, ʿAlī is able to visit Imām ʿAskarī (ʿa) as well.

"My son will be the Imām after my death," Imām ʿAskarī (ʿa) tells him when they meet. "He will be known as the Qāʾim. The tyrants of his time will force him to go into hiding, but it will all be part of Allah's plan. His ghaybah will be a difficult time for our Shīʿah, because he will not be physically present among them. But it will be Allah's way of testing the Shīʿah to see who will remain strong in their faith and work hard to prepare for their Imām's return."

From that day forward until his death, ʿAlī spreads the word about the coming of Imām Mahdī (ʿaj). He does his best to prepare the Shīʿah for a time when they will not be able to contact their Imām (ʿaj). He warns them of the trials that lie ahead, but he also shows them how to pave the way for the Imām's return.

As the Shīʿah of today, we live in that "difficult time" Imām ʿAskarī (ʿa) described to ʿAlī ibn Mahziyār hundreds of years ago. And it is our responsibility to remain strong in our faith and prepare for Imām Mahdī's return.

CHAPTER 17

Tutor to Martyr

Ibn as-Sikkīt (Yaʿqūb ibn Isḥāq)

The masjid is packed. Ẓuhr and ʿAṣr were prayed hours ago, but the prayer hall is still full. About half of the crowd is clearly students, arranged in neat rows, ready to take notes. But the other half includes all sorts of people, both young and old, who have come to listen as well. Everyone stands up out of respect when Ibn as-Sikkīt enters, and the hall is filled with a chorus of "salāmun ʿalaykum" and other warm greetings. Once the crowd settles down, the well-known scholar and much-loved teacher begins to speak.

"In the name of Allah, the All-Beneficent, the All-Merciful—" He stops. There are loud voices outside the masjid door. They don't sound like they belong to the kind of people who are willing to listen and learn.

The doors burst open, and a wave of terror ripples through the gathering. Standing in the doorway is a group of soldiers who clearly mean business.

Without any word of apology or introduction, the commander roars, "Which of you is Ibn as-Sikkīt?"

The crowd is silent, but Ibn as-Sikkīt calmly steps forward and replies, "I am."

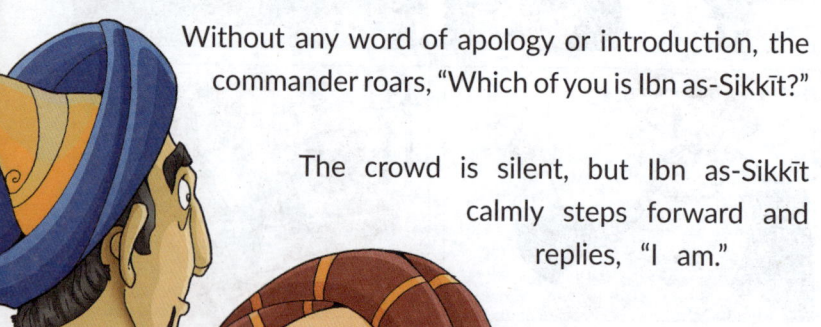

"The khalīfah of the Abbasid empire, Mutawakkil, summons you to his court in Baghdad," the commander says imperiously, apparently unable to lower his voice.

"Baghdad?" Ibn as-Sikkīt asks. "Why?"

"He wants you to teach his sons, Muʿtazz and Muʿayyad. He has heard lots of people praise you as a man of knowledge and learning, and he has decided that his children must have the best tutor in all the Muslim lands."

Ibn as-Sikkīt is disgusted, especially by the commander's obvious lack of manners. "And if I do not come?" he asks. They stand face to face. It is a challenge.

The commander draws his sword in answer to the challenge. "Do you have a choice?"

Some of the students manage to swallow their fear and rush to Ibn as-Sikkīt's defense. They try to shield their teacher with their own bodies, but the commander brandishes his sword at them threateningly.

"Don't give me any trouble," he says to Ibn as-Sikkīt. "My men are not afraid to use their weapons. If you come quietly, no one will get hurt. If not..." He looks long and hard at the people trapped in the masjid, petrified with fear.

"You will hurt no one," Ibn as-Sikkīt says sharply, raising his voice for the first time. "I will come quietly." He turns to face the terrified crowd and tries to calm them. "Wait here until the soldiers leave with me. For your own safety, don't get in their way. I will be fine, inshā'Allāh."

With a heavy heart, Ibn as-Sikkīt leads the soldiers to his home—at swordpoint. When his wife opens the door for him, she gasps. "Ibn as-Sikkīt, who are these men?" she whispers once he is inside. The soldiers insist that the door be left open, but Ibn as-Sikkīt makes sure they don't come in.

"I have a new job," he says quietly while packing up his few belongings as quickly as he can. "Mutawakkil wants me to teach his children in Baghdad. He wants me to leave immediately. I'm sorry," he adds with a sigh. "I'm sorry that I have to leave you."

"Just be careful," his wife says. "Stay safe." Ibn as-Sikkīt knows she isn't just worried for his life, but for his faith as well. Mutawakkil is a dangerous man not just because he is brutal, but because he is devious and sly.

"Thank you. I'll do my best. Keep me in your prayers." He hugs his wife tightly one last time before hoisting his pack onto his back and walking out the door to where the soldiers are waiting to take him away.

Ibn as-Sikkīt's arrival in Baghdad is very different from the way he was invited. Though he is still heavily guarded by the soldiers of the same arrogant commander, the people show him great respect and welcome him to the city. He has been to Baghdad before; in fact, he has traveled throughout the Muslim lands, and his name is widely known in these parts. He often wonders if he really deserves all these honors, and he constantly prays to Allah to protect him from arrogance. Besides, what is his fame worth if it has made a tyrant interested in hiring him as a tutor for his children?

He dreads standing before the khalīfah. He doesn't know if he will be able to control his anger. Mutawakkil is a tyrant who has only ever shown enmity toward Ibn as-Sikkīt's beloved teachers—Imām Jawād (ʿa) and Imām Hādī (ʿa). It's insulting that he now wants to make Ibn as-Sikkīt work for him. *Doesn't he know where my allegiance lies?* Ibn as-Sikkīt thinks to himself. *Is this his idea of a joke? A cruel, twisted joke?*

Of course, there's no way to escape the khalīfah. Soon after Ibn as-Sikkīt enters Baghdad, he is summoned to Mutawakkil's court to receive his official assignment. He stands silently waiting for the empty throne in front of him to be filled by a man, who, in his mind, doesn't deserve the grand title of "khalīfah".

He takes a moment to size up his surroundings. He is not dazzled by the splendor of the palace, with all its finely woven rugs, rich tapestries, and plush cushions. Nor is he impressed by the beauty of the city itself, with its carefully planned boulevards and sparkling fountains. He knows that the source of all this wealth is oppression, and the guards lurking around every corner, stationed on every rooftop and balcony, remind him of this reality.

Just then, the "khalīfah" enters, along with his two sons and a train of advisors and courtiers.

"Well, well, well," Mutawakkil says with a mocking smile as

he makes himself comfortable on his throne. "The famous Ibn as-Sikkīt. You should be thanking me. I've just made you even more famous and important. Now, you are the royal tutor of the house of Mutawakkil, ruler of the Abbasid empire. You have the great honor of teaching my sons, Muʿtazz and Muʿayyad. I trust you will give them a good education." He gestures to the two young boys who sit on either side of him.

Ibn as-Sikkīt looks evenly at Mutawakkil and nods slightly. He would much rather meet his future students than waste time with a man who is so full of himself. Still, he knows that he must respond politely, whether he likes it or not. "Education means different things to different people," he says. "Are there any subjects in particular that you would like me to focus on?"

"Teach them grammar. And literature. And poetry," Mutawakkil says. "All in Arabic, of course. I want my sons to master the subtleties of the Arabic language."

Again, Ibn as-Sikkīt nods, keeping a perfectly straight face. Although he is originally from Iran, he has studied Arabic so well and in such detail that people say he knows Arabic better than Arabs themselves. He is known to blow Arabs away with his powerful, inspiring poetry. Again, Ibn as-Sikkīt wonders if such fame is more of a blessing or a test, especially since it has brought him here.

"You can leave now," Mutawakkil says dismissively. "I expect you to be ready to begin work tomorrow."

With a last, very small nod, Ibn as-Sikkīt turns and leaves. He is followed by a pair of soldiers who escort him to his room.

Once he is alone in his room (with soldiers right outside his door), Ibn as-Sikkīt tries to figure out his first impressions of the two boys, Muʿtazz and Muʿayyad. He fights against the urge to think badly of them because of their wicked father. He tells himself that they are young, and that there is still hope for them. Perhaps he can guide them and show them where their father went wrong.

He pictures the two boys in his mind, the way he saw them in the courtroom. They were neat and well-dressed, with pleasant-looking faces, but he couldn't read their expressions. Even now, in his memory, their faces are unreadable. So far, he has no way of seeing past the surface and into their souls—which means he can't make any judgements, yet.

They were very quiet as well. They didn't speak a word. Maybe they were scared. For a moment, Ibn as-Sikkīt imagines what it must be like to be in their place. What is it like to have a tyrant for a father? Maybe they are frightened, afraid to displease him, and so they have no choice but to obey him.

It softens Ibn as-Sikkīt's heart to think about the boys as children instead of heirs to the Abbasid throne. He is surprised at how young they are, not even bāligh. Maybe he can help them and save them from the evil of their own father.

Teaching Muʿtazz and Muʿayyad is easy and complicated at

the same time. Ibn as-Sikkīt has no complaints about them as students. They are well-behaved and quick to learn. But it is hard to really measure their progress. For one thing, they don't ask many questions. At first, they asked almost no questions at all. Instead of them just not being curious, Ibn as-Sikkīt suspects that they are afraid.

So, for the most part, he sticks to the lesson plan and treats them how he would treat any of his students. He is patient and kind, but it is hard to show them love and affection. While he can see that they have healthy, active minds, he cannot see into their hearts. He blocks unfair thoughts from creeping into his mind, making sure not to blame them for what their father has done. Still, he is worried about what they might grow up to do.

When they grow up, what's to stop them from being as ruthless as their father? What's to stop them from murdering his beloved Imāms like the Abbasid rulers before them? Ibn as-Sikkīt can't help but think these thoughts. Even though he has always enjoyed teaching, he is never able to fully enjoy teaching these boys. He performs his duties to the best of his ability, but his heart isn't in it.

He asks himself, Isn't it my job, as a teacher, to shape my

students' minds and help them to grow into good Muslims? It's true that he's doing the job he was assigned by teaching them grammar, literature, and poetry, and Mutawakkil is satisfied with that, but is he really helping the children with that sort of education? Is he steering them away from evil and toward good? Or is he just helping them on their way to become well-read, intelligent leaders who are also evil and ruthless, just like their father? Shouldn't he be doing more to guide them—to help them discover their talents and use them in service of their Imām (ʿa)?

A child doesn't have to choose the same path as his parents. Ibn as-Sikkīt knows the story of Khālid ibn Saʿīd ibn al-ʿĀs, who opposed his father and accepted the Prophet's message in the early days of Islam. He also knows the story of Saʿd al-Khayr (or "the good Saʿd") a close companion of Imām Ṣādiq (ʿa) who rejected the ways of his evil Umayyad forefathers and was accepted as part of the Ahl al-Bayt (ʿa). There is still hope that these boys will change! But how can he do it without making Mutawakkil suspicious? And how will the boys respond? Will they listen? Is there any point?

After spending a long time wrestling with these questions, Ibn as-Sikkīt begins to form a new kind of lesson plan. He decides that he will slowly sneak teachings of the Imāms (ʿa) into his regular lessons. He will do what he can to introduce the boys to the wisdom of his dear teachers and true masters. What they do in the end—whether they follow the path of the Imāms (ʿa) or their father—is up to them.

One day, Ibn as-Sikkīt takes a break from the main lesson of the day and asks his two students if they would like to hear a story. Politely, they say yes, but they look puzzled. Ibn as-Sikkīt guesses that they probably haven't heard many stories; their father doesn't seem like the kind of person who tells his children bedtime stories before they sleep.

"What I'm about to tell you isn't exactly poetry or literature, but it is still very important. Lots of times, stories are the best ways to learn. They can teach us lessons that help us become better people.

"This story is about two brothers, maybe a little bit younger than the two of you. One day, just before the Ẓuhr adhān, these brothers come to a small pool to do wuḍūʾ. Just then, an old man comes to the pool and begins to do wuḍūʾ as well. The boys watch him quietly. They notice that the old man makes a few mistakes in the way he performs wuḍūʾ, and they want to correct him—kindly and respectfully. So they come up with a plan. They start arguing between themselves about the correct way to do wuḍūʾ, which draws the old man's attention. He walks up to them and offers to watch while they each take turns doing wuḍūʾ to decide who is right and who is wrong. As he watches, he sees that the two boys do wuḍūʾ in exactly the same way, and when he looks closely at their faces, he realizes who they are. Then, he realizes that he was the one who was doing wuḍūʾ incorrectly, and that the two boys were trying to find a way to show him this without hurting his feelings. He kisses the two boys and thanks them for pointing out his mistake so gently. Afterward, they walk together toward the masjid for prayer."

"Who were the two boys?" Muʿayyad asks after the story is over.

"Their names were Ḥasan and Ḥusayn. Their father was ʿAlī, son of Abū Ṭālib; and their mother was Fāṭimah, daughter of the Prophet (ṣ)."

That night, Muʿayyad gathers the courage to ask, "Father, do you know anything about two brothers named Ḥasan and Ḥusayn?" It is an innocent question, but Mutawakkil's face darkens.

"How do you know those names?" he demands.

"I...I... just heard someone talking about them," Muʿayyad stammers, "and... I... I wanted to know who they were."

"They are nobody," Mutawakkil says harshly. "I never want to hear you mention them again."

"Yes, Father," Muʿayyad whispers. He hurries to bed, leaving his father alone in the room.

Mutawakkil takes a deep breath and folds his arms. He is glad that he's kept a close eye on the new tutor. He knew something like this might happen—that Ibn as-Sikkīt would try to turn his children against him with unwelcome ideas about the children of ʿAlī (ʿa). In fact, he is surprised that it took so long for Ibn as-Sikkīt to show his true colors.

It's a shame to get rid of such a distinguished teacher, Mutawakkil thinks, but he can't let his children be exposed to such dangerous ideas. His lips curl in a wicked smile as he forms a plan. He will give Ibn as-Sikkīt a choice: he must renounce his love for the Ahl al-Bayt (ʿa) or die.

To Mutawakkil, it's an easy choice. Of course, any sane man would value his own life over loyalty to someone else. He thinks this is the perfect way to crush Ibn as-Sikkīt and bully him into rejecting the Imāms (ʿa). He doesn't understand how anything can be more valuable than wealth and fame. He thinks he can scare Ibn as-Sikkīt with death. He underestimates Ibn as-Sikkīt's love for the Imāms (ʿa), and it never crosses his mind that the world-famous scholar would be willing to sacrifice everything—his job, his reputation, his life—for those Imāms.

The next day, Mutawakkil summons Ibn as-Sikkīt to his court.

"If you are to continue teaching my sons, I need to know where your true loyalties lie," he says. "I know you consider yourself a lover of the children of ʿAlī. Let's see how strong your love is, if you love them more than you value your own life. Tell me," he says, his eyes glittering dangerously. "Ḥasan and Ḥusayn." He spits out the names. "Are they more dear to you, or my sons?"

Ibn as-Sikkīt's life flashes before his eyes. He

remembers his teachers—Imām Jawād (ʿa) and Imām Hādī (ʿa)—and everything they've taught him. He thinks about everything he's learned about the Ahl al-Bayt (ʿa) and everything that they have done for the Muslim ummah. Mutawakkil's shameless question fills Ibn as-Sikkīt with rage. How dare he ask such a question! Does he know the status of Ḥasan (ʿa) and Ḥusayn (ʿa)? How dare he compare the best of Allah's creation to his own sons, while it remains to be seen if they will choose the path of good or evil!

When he responds, Ibn as-Sikkīt's voice rings out fearlessly through the courtroom, astonishing everyone who is present. "Allah is my witness that Qanbar, ʿAlī's loyal servant, is more dear to me than your sons, let alone Ḥasan and Ḥusayn, the grandsons of Allah's Messenger!"

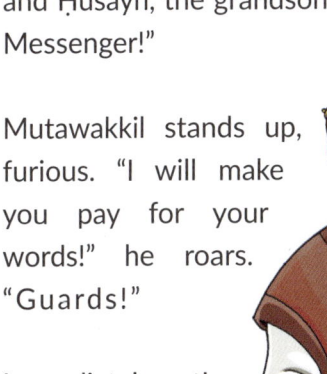

Mutawakkil stands up, furious. "I will make you pay for your words!" he roars. "Guards!"

Immediately, the guards standing

by the doorways surround Ibn as-Sikkīt.

“Take him away,” Mutawakkil orders, “and punish him.”

The guards drag Ibn as-Sikkīt out of the room. He does not protest or resist. He looks Mutawakkil fearlessly in the eye until he is out of sight.

Outside, he hardly feels the guard’s vicious blows as they strike his body. He feels like a great weight has slipped off his shoulders. No more pretending. No more hiding his faith. He hopes he has passed Allah’s test by staying true to his values and remaining loyal to the Imāms (ʿa) until his last breath.

With his last ounce of strength, he gasps, “There is no god but Allah. Muḥammad is His Messenger. ʿAlī is the Prophet’s rightful successor,” right before Allah takes his soul.

CHAPTER 18

One Teacher, Many Blessings

Faḍl ibn Shādhān

Nishapur glows with the freshness of spring. Everything is young and green and full of new life. Faḍl ibn Shādhān walks side by side with his young student as they cross a newly plowed field.

"Tomorrow, I will leave for Samarra, inshā'Allāh. I wanted to see you and talk with you one last time before I leave," the young man says. "After everything that you've taught me about the Imāms, I can't stop thinking about them. I love them as if they were my own teachers, and I feel like I can't wait any longer to visit the Imām of our time, Imām 'Askarī ('a)."

Faḍl smiles. "Ḥāmid, seeing your love for the Imām makes me love him even more. I'm glad you have this opportunity to visit him. Please send him my salāms."

"Of course,"

Ḥāmid promises. He is silent for a moment. Then he asks, "What is it like, meeting the Imām?"

"It's beyond what words can describe," Faḍl says with a faraway look in his eyes. "When you meet him, you'll understand what I mean."

For Ḥāmid, Samarra is a bittersweet sight, just like it is for all Shīʿah who come in the hopes of meeting Imām ʿAskarī (ʿa). While his heart flutters with excitement over being so close to the Imām (ʿa), it is painful to see the harsh conditions in which he is forced to live. He is under heavy surveillance, not allowed to leave his own house, and there are soldiers everywhere.

This makes it difficult for the Shīʿah to visit him, but when a people's love for their leader and guide is strong enough, they will find ways to make possible what seems impossible. Ḥāmid knows this, and so he quickly takes the necessary steps. He manages to contact a friend who has important connections with some of the guards. With a little bit of help, disguised in a soldier's uniform, he slips past the guards unnoticed and enters the Imām's home.

Ḥāmid stands near the doorway, uncomfortable under an extra layer of clothing. A servant passes by, carrying a water jug. He takes one look at Ḥāmid, dressed like a soldier, and gives a small cry of alarm.

"Don't worry—I'm not one of them," Ḥāmid says quickly. "This was the only way I could meet the Imām. I'm sorry if I startled you. I know things must be very hard for all of you in this household."

Visibly relieved, the servant gives a small smile. "I know I should be used to this by now. You're not the first one to use that trick. But some habits are hard to change. If you follow me, I can take you to my master."

"Let me take this off first," Ḥāmid says, pulling off his borrowed uniform.

After meeting the Imām (ʿa), Ḥāmid realizes that his teacher was right. It is an experience beyond words. The Imām (ʿa) carries himself with a quiet dignity, but he is also humble and down-to-earth, which puts Ḥāmid at ease. Even though his knowledge outmatches that of anyone around him, he speaks at the same level as the person he is speaking to. Talking with him is like talking to a wise and patient friend. On top of all that, despite the fact that he is held prisoner in his own home by the evil khalīfah, he is still full of energy, and his face shines with a nobility purer and greater than that of any king. He welcomes Ḥāmid with a cheerful smile and is a kind and generous host.

Ḥāmid and the Imām (ʿa) talk with each other late into the afternoon and even into early evening. Ḥāmid realizes with a jolt that he must get going while there is still light outside.

"My Imām, I really wish I could stay longer, but I must leave before dark," he says, with a wistful look in his eyes. It is clear that he is reluctant to leave the Imām's side. "Besides, I would hate to put you in any danger by staying here any longer."

"I'm afraid you're right," the Imām (ʿa) says. "After sunset, no one is allowed to enter or leave my home. I would ask you to stay the night, but they'll come in to inspect all the rooms and make sure there's no one here except me and my family." The

Imām (ʿa) sounds tired, but he smiles and stands up. "Let me walk you to the door. We still have a few minutes together."

As Ḥāmid stands to leave, something slides out from the bundle of uniform in his arms and falls to the floor. It is a book. The Imām (ʿa) bends to pick it up and smooths out the crumpled pages.

"It is one of my teacher's books—Faḍl ibn Shādhān," Ḥāmid says. He suddenly remembers his promise to Faḍl; in all the excitement since coming to Samarra, he'd forgotten his teacher's request. "He sends you his salāms."

"May Allah bless Faḍl. He has been a loyal companion to both me and my father," the Imām (ʿa) says as he hands the book back to Ḥāmid. "The people of Khorasan are blessed to have a scholar like him among them. There are very few people who are as careful as he is when recording ḥadīth.

He is the

kind of person you know you can trust completely. Ḥāmid, you have a treasure trove of knowledge at your fingertips. Never forget what a blessing it is to have a teacher like Faḍl."

Ḥāmid nods. He thanks the Imām (ʿa) for his hospitality and good advice and slips out of the Imām's house as stealthily as he came.

On his return journey, Ḥāmid replays the Imām's parting words over and over in his head. After hearing the Imām's praise of Faḍl, Ḥāmid sees the value of his teacher more clearly than ever before. He worries that perhaps he didn't show enough appreciation for everything that Faḍl had done for him in the past, and he promises himself that from now on, he will not take his kind and patient tutor for granted.

Back in Nishapur, Ḥāmid sees how much the community depends on Faḍl for guidance and advice. People travel from all over to study with him, and he takes them under his wing as students. He follows in the footsteps of his forefathers by devoting himself to serving the Imāms and spreading their teachings. In particular, he constantly reminds his students about the 12th Imām, Imām Mahdī (ʿaj). He explains that

Allah will make Imām Mahdī (ʿaj) enter the ghaybah to keep him safe from his enemies, and that the Imām (ʿaj) will remain hidden until his Shīʿah prove that they are ready for his return.

One day, a man named Sahl asks Faḍl, "How long have you been studying, recording, and teaching the ḥadīth of the Maʿṣūmīn (ʿa)?"

Faḍl replies with a smile, "I am just a part of a great tradition of scholars that has existed long before me. For decades, these scholars have fought against the enemies of the Ahl al-Bayt (ʿa) by educating the public and exposing lies with the truth. My life's work is just one drop in a vast sea of knowledge."

The man is silent for a moment as he reflects on the humility of Faḍl's response. Then he says, "May Allah reward your efforts, and may all the students you have trained continue this great legacy, inshāʾAllāh!"

Ḥāmid is only one of the many students Faḍl has inspired. Būraq is another young man who has come to love the Imāms and the Ahl al-Bayt (ʿa) because of what he has learned from his teacher. Now, like Ḥāmid, he wants to visit Imām ʿAskarī (ʿa) in person, and he has come to thank his teacher and bid him farewell before leaving for Samarra.

"Is there anything I can do for you after everything you've done for me?" Būraq asks Faḍl. "I wouldn't be going on this journey if it wasn't for you."

"There is one thing," Faḍl says slowly. For a second, his words slur together with age. Then his expression clears. "I have a book of ḥadīth I just finished compiling, but before I share it with others, I want to make sure I haven't included anything false by mistake. When you go to visit the Imām, will you take it to him and ask him to check it for any errors I may have made?"

"Of course," says Būraq. "I pray that I'm able to bring your book back to you, safe and sound."

The situation in Samarra isn't any better when Būraq arrives. The Imām ('a) is still under house arrest, and his neighborhood looks like a military base instead of a pleasant place to live. But, just like Ḥāmid and so many others, Būraq finds a way to meet with the Imām ('a). This time, he takes the place of a servant who was sent to the market for some food and enters the Imām's home carrying a basket full of bread and dates.

The Imām ('a) welcomes Būraq inside, and they sit and talk for several hours. Before asking permission to leave, Būraq remembers his teacher's book. He takes it out of his bag and offers it to the Imām ('a).

"This is a book written by my teacher," he says. "He wanted your approval before sharing it with others to avoid any risk of misguiding people by mistake."

"Faḍl has always been careful about separating what is false from what is true," the Imām ('a) says approvingly. "We need more teachers like him who will further strengthen Shī'ah scholarship and learning. If you leave the book with me tonight, I will read it, inshāʾAllāh. Do you think you'll be able to come back tomorrow morning?"

"Inshāʾ Allāh," Būraq replies, "with the help of the One who helped me the first time."

Būraq returns late the next morning, just a little while before Ẓuhr. The Imām (ʿa) hands the book to him, smiling.

"Faḍl did his work well," he says. "I pray this book will be a lantern that helps guide many people. If people sincerely act on the wisdom found within these pages, it will help bring them closer and closer to Allah."

As Būraq tucks the book back into

his bag, the Imām's smile suddenly vanishes, replaced by an expression of grief and pain. "May Allah bless Faḍl," he murmurs to himself, along with some other prayers under his breath which Būraq does not hear. Then he turns to Būraq and says, "Follow in the footsteps of your teacher," before walking him to the door.

When Būraq returns to Nishapur, before going to his own home, he goes first to his teacher's house so he can return the book. On his way, he bumps into one of his friends who used to study with him.

"Salāmun ʿalaykum, Būraq," his friend says. There is sadness in his smile. "You look like you've just come back; you probably haven't heard the news—our teacher, Faḍl, is no longer with us in this world. Allah took his soul while you were away."

Tears blur Būraq's vision. "When did this happen?" he asks, his voice wobbly. "Do you remember the day?"

Būraq's friend replies with the date. "It was just around Ẓuhr time," he adds.

Būraq is still. For a moment, he closes his eyes. In his mind, he sees Imām ʿAskarī's smile fade to a frown followed by a quiet, murmured prayer: "May Allah bless Faḍl." That had happened on the same day, even around the same time...

It is no coincidence. Even as Būraq grieves for his noble teacher, he is full of wonder at the Imām's knowledge of the unseen. Although Samarra and Nishapur are over a thousand miles apart, the Imām (ʿa) had known the exact moment of Faḍl's death. His parting words ring in Būraq's ears as he realizes their true meaning: "Follow in the footsteps of your teacher."

"Inshāʾ Allāh," Būraq whispers, clutching his teacher's book to his chest. "With Allah's help, I will try my very best to continue your legacy."

Epilogue

Because of the extreme oppression that the Shīʿah faced in early Islamic history, it was often difficult to study and document ḥadīth. As a result, the knowledge of the Ahl al-Bayt (ʿa) that has reached us today is not as vast as it could have been had books of ḥadīth not been destroyed and scholars not been oppressed.

In order to recover from this disadvantage, whenever a possibility presented itself, companions such as Faḍl worked with enthusiasm, courage, and vigour, to preserve the teachings of the Ahl al-Bayt (ʿa) and document them. In this way, Faḍl strengthened the foundation of Islamic knowledge that we have today, as Āyatullāh Khoei praised in one of his speeches.

May Allah bless Faḍl for his hard work and dedication. We need to appreciate the work of our scholars, both past and present, who have dedicated their lives to carrying on the legacy of the Ahl al-Bayt (ʿa). We must not let their efforts be in vain by benefiting from their knowledge and following in their scholarly footsteps.

CHAPTER 19

A Secret Birth

Aḥmad ibn Isḥāq al-Ashʿarī

By mid-morning, the streets of Qom are bustling with activity. Shop owners tidy up their stores and arrange their goods in all sorts of creative ways, hoping to catch the eye of anyone who walks past. Already, a few potential customers stroll past the busy storefronts, admiring the displays.

A messenger weaves his way through the marketplace, a bag full of letters slung over his shoulder. He turns into a quiet alley until he comes to a row of four houses. Then, he stops. He knows he has to deliver a letter to someone in one of these houses, but he doesn't know which one.

Just then, the door to the middle house swings open, and an older man steps outside, his beard silvery with grey hairs. After greeting him, the messenger asks, "Are you Aḥmad ibn Isḥāq? I was told that he lived on this street, but I don't know which house is his."

Aḥmad returns the greeting and replies with a smile, "Yes, I am Aḥmad. You have come to the right place."

"It's an honor to meet you. On my visits, I've met many people here in Qom who look up to you as their teacher and mentor," the messenger says, pulling something out of his bag. "I have a letter for you. Whatever might be inside, I think it's urgent. I made sure to deliver it as quickly as possible. Inshā'Allāh nothing is wrong."

Aḥmad takes the letter and turns it over in his hands. "Thank you," he says.

The messenger respectfully bows his head. "It was my pleasure. If you'll excuse me, I need to deliver some more letters in the area. Salāmun ʿalaykum."

"Wa ʿalaykum salām."

As the messenger hurries away, Aḥmad eagerly opens the letter. The word "urgent" makes him uneasy, and he wonders what kind of news he will find inside. A waft of some lovely perfume fills the air. Aḥmad quickly glances at the bottom of the page to see who it

is from, and his heart fills with warmth and joy. It is a letter from Imām Ḥasan al-ʿAskarī (ʿa):

Salāmun ʿalaykum dearest Aḥmad,

Alḥamdulillāh, my son has been born. I wanted you to know right away so that you can share in our joy. But this is a secret you must guard with your life from those who want to harm us. Only tell those whom you know you can trust. Though I know it is a long and difficult journey from Qom to Samarra, please come visit us whenever you can. Then I can explain everything to you, inshāʾAllāh.

Was salām

"Alḥamdulillāh," Aḥmad whispers, his eyes stinging with tears of joy.

For years, he has been waiting for this news—ever since Imām ʿAskarī (ʿa) had said to him, "Inshāʾ Allah, when the time comes, you will meet my son who will be the Imām after me. He will be known as the Qāʾim, and he will establish truth and justice throughout the world."

Almost faint with happiness, Aḥmad sits down on his doorstep. He feels like he has been holding his breath all this time—without even realizing it—waiting for the glad tidings of the birth of the last Imām (ʿaj). Now, he can finally breathe again.

He lets his mind slip down memory lane to his younger days, when he had met Imām Jawād (ʿa) and Imām Hādī (ʿa). Then, he brings himself back to the present and raises his hands in duʿā. Sitting on his doorstep, Imām ʿAskarī's letter in his lap, Aḥmad thanks Allah for adding the promise of meeting Imām Mahdī (ʿaj) to the triple blessing of meeting three Imāms during a single lifetime.

As soon as he can, Aḥmad makes preparations to travel to Samarra. As he bids farewell to his students, his family, and his friends, he reminds them of the coming of the Qāʾim, the 12th and final Imām (ʿaj).

"We must have faith in his return even when we cannot see him," he advises them. "We must show what we are willing to sacrifice for him. We must show him that we are ready. And we must ask ourselves, 'When the time comes, will we pledge our allegiance to him? Will we be ready to lay down our lives for him?'"

The people of Qom are eager to show their enthusiasm and demonstrate their devotion. They come to Aḥmad and ask him to take their gifts to Imām ʿAskarī (ʿa). Many people come with a gift in one hand and a slip of paper in the other—either a question or a simple message for the Imām (ʿa).

Aḥmad's saddlebags quickly fill with gifts, questions, and expressions of loyalty and love. After a final farewell and a few final hugs, he is on his way.

When Aḥmad arrives at Samarra, he acts like an ordinary messenger in order to avoid drawing any attention to himself, though he is visibly older than most messengers. If any of the Abbasid soldiers decide to inspect his bags, they will only see rolls of parchment and paper with ordinary, unimportant

messages—nothing suspicious. But buried under those papers are the letters and gifts he has brought from Qom for Imām ʿAskarī (ʿa).

It doesn't take long for him to convince the guards that surround Imām ʿAskarī's home to let him inside. He explains to them that his visit might be longer than usual because many of the letters had gotten mixed up. After allowing them to rummage through his bags and examine a few of the fake letters, ʿAḥmad is able to enter the Imām's home.

"Salāmun ʿalaykum, Aḥmad! I am very glad you came." Imām ʿAskarī (ʿa) greets Aḥmad with a warm smile.

"Wa ʿalaykum salām, my Imām," Aḥmad replies. He is always amazed by the Imām's cheerful contentment despite the harsh circumstances he lives in. Today, however, the Imām (ʿa) radiates even more happiness than usual. Aḥmad thinks he knows why. "Congratulations on the birth of your son!" he says. "I keep thanking Allah that I am alive to see this day. Ever since you told me about the Qāʾim, I have been praying to catch a glimpse of his face. When I received your letter, I came as quickly as I could."

Imām ʿAskarī (ʿa) invites Aḥmad into another room to sit down. Aḥmad brings with him the bags of letters and gifts. Together, they discuss the situation of the Shīʿah.

"How are the Shīʿah in Qom?" the Imām (ʿa) asks. "How is their faith in the Qāʾim? Do you think they are ready for the challenging times to come?"

"As you might tell from these gifts, they are very eager to prove their love and loyalty, but we have not been tested yet," Aḥmad says truthfully. "I can't predict how they will react to whatever difficulties we may face. Inshāʾ Allāh their faith will be just as strong in hardship as it is in ease."

The Imām (ʿa) nods. "Inshāʾ Allāh. We must do what we can to prepare them for the stormy times ahead. Since the creation of man, Allah has always placed a guide on Earth, and every guide has had a successor, one after another. There has never been a moment in time when there was no guide present, and there never will be. This holds true for my son during his ghaybah as well. Even though he will be forced to go into hiding because of the cruelty of the Abbasids, he will not abandon the people. He will be hidden from view, but his heart will be right alongside those who believe in him.

"It is crucial that the Shīʿah know this—that they will not be alone during the separation that is to come. Otherwise, they will lose hope and lose faith, and our cause will collapse."

"I will do my best to prepare the people of my city," Aḥmad promises.

The Imām (ʿa) rises to his feet. Aḥmad is about to rise with him when the Imām (ʿa) motions for him to sit back down. "Rest a little after your journey. I'll return in a few moments."

Imām ʿAskarī (ʿa) returns with a white bundle cradled in his arms. It is a baby, swaddled in a blanket. His face glows like the moon. Aḥmad's breath gets caught in his chest as he approaches the 12th and final Imām, Muḥammad al-Mahdī (ʿaj).

His whole body trembling, Aḥmad bends to kiss the infant's forehead. The grey hairs of his beard brush against a soft cheek. His face reflects the newborn Imām's light like a mirror.

Then Imām ʿAskarī (ʿa) speaks again. "Aḥmad, you have always been a loyal follower and friend of the Ahl al-Bayt. This is why I have shown you my successor. The rest of my followers need to know about him as well, but I cannot announce it freely because I fear for his life. The Abbasid khalīfah will kill him if he finds out he exists. Can I trust you to cautiously spread the word?"

"Of course," Aḥmad says, bowing his head. Then he lifts his gaze and looks deep into the infant's eyes. They are wide and alert, sparkling with both a child's innocence and the wisdom of an Imām. Just as Aḥmad is about to look away, the baby smiles. His tiny face lights up with joy and melts Aḥmad's heart.

Imām ʿAskarī (ʿa) watches this tender exchange with a smile. "I know you have been waiting a long time for this moment," he says to Aḥmad. "The Shīʿah have another long wait ahead of them. This child will complete the mission of the great-grandfather whose name he bears, and he will fill the earth with justice. But Allah will first test the Muslim ummah to measure the strength of its faith. The Shīʿah must prove that they are ready before the Qāʾim will return from the ghaybah. He needs to be confident that his supporters will never desert him, no matter what, otherwise it will not be safe for him to lead them. If the Shīʿah want to taste the Qāʾim's victory, they must first work toward making his return possible."

The Imām (ʿa) pauses for a moment. Then he gently places his son in Aḥmad's arms and says, "Aḥmad, you have seen the Imām after me. You are holding him in your arms. Do not forget this moment. Use it to anchor yourself in what is real and true. I promise you that if you continue to hold fast to the truth, you will be raised with us on Resurrection Day."

Aḥmad feels the weight of the infant in his arms. This child is his anchor. This child is the hope of humankind. This child will grow to spread justice to every corner of the world. And yet, he is small enough that he disappears in the folds of Aḥmad's sleeves as he hugs him to his chest. The baby's blankets are wet with Aḥmad's tears after his farewell embrace.

Aḥmad returns home with his saddlebags much emptier than when he left, but his heart is full of Imām ʿAskarī's words of advice and encouragement—the Imām's gift to his Shīʿah in Qom.

The memory of the young Imām Mahdī's face gives Aḥmad strength as he conveys Imām ʿAskarī's messages to the people. He spreads the glad tidings of Allah's promise and shows the people what they must do for Allah to make that promise a reality. He thanks Allah for the deep sense of fulfillment he feels in his old age. He is at peace.

Until the time of his death, he reminds his students, friends, and family to be strong during the ghaybah. He repeats to them Imām ʿAskarī's words of comfort: that they will not be alone; that Imām Mahdī (ʿaj) will be hidden from view, but his heart will be right alongside those who believe in him.

When the Angel of Death comes for him, Aḥmad is not afraid. He has held fast to the truth. On Resurrection Day, he knows where he will stand.

CHAPTER 20

The Missing Link

ʿAbdullāh ibn Jaʿfar al-Ḥimyarī

One by one, ʿAbdullāh's students file out of the masjid until only two are left: a pair of brothers who are never done asking questions.

"Shaykh Ḥimyarī," one of them begins, his notes still clutched to his chest. He uses the title that the people of Qom use to refer to his teacher. "This time, our question doesn't have to do with the lesson or the discussion. It's...it's a bigger question that we've had for a long time. Right now, we're students, and we're learning so much from you every day. I don't think I can ever get tired of learning. But sometimes, we wonder if we'll ever become like you. How long did it take you to go from being a student to being a teacher?"

ʿAbdullāh smiles. "It's taking me a long time. I'm still a student in so many ways. I have so many questions, just like you. I have to look in whatever books I have and learn

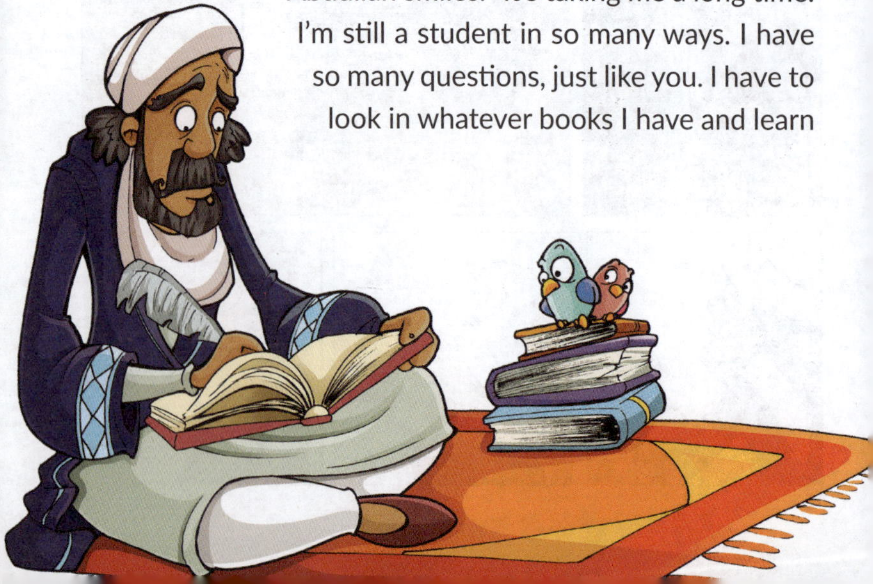

from the infinite wisdom that our Imāms (ʿa) have to share. But you don't have to stop being a student to become a teacher. Teaching can be as simple as sharing something that you've learned with someone else. What's more, when you teach someone something, it helps you remember it even better. The more you teach, the better you learn; the more you learn, the better you can teach.

"But whether we are students, teachers, or both, we have to remember that all knowledge is from Allah. No matter how much we learn, it's still nothing compared to His knowledge. Just thinking about His infinite knowledge and wisdom makes me feel very, very small." For a moment, ʿAbdullāh gazes thoughtfully into midair, forgetting that his two students are still with him.

His answer startles the two brothers. It is hard for them to imagine their great, wise teacher as "small," or even as a student. But they realize that he's right.

"Thank you," says the same brother who had spoken earlier. "We'll try to remember. It...it feels good to know that we're not the only ones who feel small when we think about everything that the Imāms know...and everything that Allah knows."

"Thank you," the other brother says with a shy smile. "Salāmun ʿalaykum, Shaykh Ḥimyarī."

"Wa ʿalaykum salām," ʿAbdullāh says, looking fondly after his students as they leave the masjid.

On his way home, ʿAbdullāh replays the advice he gave to the two brothers in his head. He told them that he often had to consult his books to refresh his memory of the Imāms' teachings. But lately, he has begun to feel like the books aren't enough. It's not enough to see the words of the Imāms (ʿa) written on paper. ʿAbdullāh longs for a deeper, more personal connection. He longs to physically renew his allegiance to his Imāms (ʿa), and, for that, he must go to Iraq.

While he has been planning to make this journey for a long time, his conversation with the two brothers has motivated him to finally take action. The road ahead is not easy, but that doesn't stop ʿAbdullāh. He decides that he will first visit the grave of Imām ʿAlī (ʿa) in Najaf and spend some time in nearby Kufa. Since Kufa is one of the centers of Muslim learning at the time, he hopes he'll be able to meet some Shīʿah scholars who can help him connect with the Ahl al-Bayt (ʿa) and their great legacy. From Kufa, he can travel to Samarra to visit Imām ʿAskarī (ʿa), just as he visited Imām Hādī (ʿa) many years ago. The very thought of meeting the Imām of his time again sends shivers of excitement down ʿAbdullāh's spine.

"Alḥamdulillāh," he murmurs to himself, bursting with gratitude to Allah for allowing him to make this journey once more during his lifetime.

Within days, ʿAbdullāh's bags are packed. While his wife and children wish very much that they could come with him, the journey is too difficult for the whole family to go on together. As he bids them farewell, ʿAbdullāh promises to convey their salāms to Imām ʿAskarī (ʿa). Then, he is on his way to Najaf. A mixture of hope and exhilaration provides him with the energy he needs to survive hundreds of miles of weary travel. As he approaches his destination, his heart thumps in his chest, and tears spring to his eyes.

Najaf is not yet a big city, but it is already blessed by a steady trickle of pilgrims. They fill the air with prayers and Qurʾān and duʿās. ʿAbdullāh feels like he is floating in a dream as he weaves his way toward Imām ʿAlī's grave. When he reaches the grave—the city's heart—ʿAbdullāh kneels beside it and kisses it. He places his palm on it and closes his eyes.

"Salāmun ʿalaykum, my Imām, the Commander of the Faithful," he whispers. "I've come to renew my pledge to you, and I beg for your prayers and blessings. Please accept this ziyārah from your humble servant!"

Kufa fills ʿAbdullāh with a different kind of amazement and admiration. The streets are teeming with students and scholars. Everywhere he looks, there are classes in session. Everyone seems to have books or scrolls tucked under their arms.

"Inshā'Allāh I've come to the right place," he says to himself. "I think I'll stay here a while. Maybe I'll find some of the answers that I'm looking for."

Before long, the blank parchment ʿAbdullāh brought with him is filled with the ḥadīth that he has learned in Kufa. In the process of collecting new ḥadīth and sharing what he knows with other scholars, he has made many good, wise friends who are more than happy to help him in his quest to reconnect with the Imāms (ʿa) and the Ahl al-Bayt (ʿa).

One day, he tells one of these friends, who has become a mentor to him, that he wants to visit Imām ʿAskarī (ʿa) in Samarra. "Can you tell me what the best way is for me to meet him?" he asks. "How bad is the situation in Samarra? Is it very different from how it was during the time of his father?"

His mentor sighs. "The situation is still very difficult in Samarra, both for our Imām (ʿa) and for the Shīʿah who want to visit him. He is guarded by the soldiers of the Abbasid khalīfah, Muʿtamid, day and night. But it is possible to meet him. I have a friend in Samarra who can help you when you get there."

"Thank you," ʿAbdullāh says, his eyes shining. "I'd be very grateful to have your friend's help. For so many years, the people of Qom have come to me with their questions. I've taught them and their children; I've recorded ḥadīth and written books. But I've learned during that time that what I do know is nothing compared to what I do not know, and that my knowledge is worth nothing if I don't build a strong connection with Allah and His Imāms (ʿa). I hope and pray that this journey will help me strengthen that connection."

ʿAbdullāh's trip to Samarra fills him with secret joy. He no longer feels like there is something missing in his life. After meeting with Imām ʿAskarī (ʿa), he feels complete.

During his stay in Kufa, he makes a few more trips to Samarra. It is a journey of a couple hundred miles, and Samarra is certainly not a safe place for a Shīʿah to be, but ʿAbdullāh hardly notices these obstacles. The reward of meeting the Imām (ʿa) is much greater than any risk that the journey involves. Of course, he is always careful to take the proper precautions.

On one of his journeys from Kufa to Samarra, ʿAbdullāh crosses paths with a caravan that has just left Samarra and is heading in the opposite direction. When he approaches them, curious to know if they bring any news from the city, he sees grief written on their faces and sadness in their eyes.

"Salāmun ʿalaykum!" he calls out. "Do you bring any news from Samarra? Has something bad happened?"

"We're mourning the loss of a loved one," one man replies cautiously. He has no way of knowing if ʿAbdullāh is a friend or foe—if he's a friend of the Shīʿah or a friend of the khalīfah.

ʿAbdullāh's heart skips a beat. "Who is this loved one...?" he trails off and looks up in horror. "Not the Imām!"

Relief flickers across the face of the man who had spoken. ʿAbdullāh is a friend—a lover of the Ahl al-Bayt (ʿa). But the relief is immediately replaced again by pain.

"Yes," he says. His voice drops to a whisper. "He was poisoned." He doesn't need to explain who did it. ʿAbdullāh already knows—Muʿtamid.

When ʿAbdullāh arrives in Samarra, the city is in turmoil. The streets are filled with mourners, but the security around the Imām's house has more than doubled. It is clear that the people want to offer their condolences to the Imām's family, but the soldiers don't let anyone approach the house. ʿAbdullāh watches from a distance as an old man breaks free from the crowd and tries to get past the soldiers. He is outraged when the soldiers roughly shove the old man aside, making him stumble and fall to the ground.

ʿAbdullāh leans against the wall of a nearby building for support, suddenly feeling faint. His heart is torn between grief for Imām ʿAskarī's death and rage at Muʿtamid for this shameless act of murder. How could he possibly justify killing the Imām (ʿa)? All his life, Imām ʿAskarī (ʿa) helped people, guided people, and showed people kindness. Was this how the Abbasid government wanted to repay all the service the Imām (ʿa) had done for the sake of the Muslim ummah?

Deeply shaken, ʿAbdullāh wanders through the street of Samarra in a daze. His feet automatically avoid crowds of

upset people or anything that could potentially mean trouble. Since traveling from Qom to visit Najaf, Kufa, and Samarra, he has been able to feed his soul with much needed nourishment. Near Imām ʿAlī's shrine and in the presence of Imām ʿAskarī (ʿa), ʿAbdullāh was able to find what he missed so intensely back home in Qom. He was able to build a closer relationship with both the Imām of his time and the Imāms (ʿa) before him. Now, with Imām ʿAskarī's martyrdom, he feels like everything he worked to build is shattered. He feels lost again, just when he thought he had found his way.

By evening, ʿAbdullāh's tired legs end up leading him in a wide circle, and he stands in front of the Imām's house again. Soldiers still stand guard, but it is quieter now. He gazes wistfully at the closed door. If only he could go in...

He thinks back to his last meeting with the Imām (ʿa), trying to call to mind every last shred of guidance he had ever shared, searching for a final warning or a farewell piece of advice.

All of a sudden, one image comes sharply into focus: the face of a young boy, not even five years old. The face of the Qāʾim (ʿaj).

As that face flashes through his mind, ʿAbdullāh remembers what Imām ʿAskarī (ʿa) had told him about his son. He remembers the late Imām (ʿa) explaining the dire need for secrecy; how the pregnancy of his wife, Lady Narjis, was miraculously kept hidden; how only a handful of his most trusted companions knew of the child's birth; how that child would one day be the Imām after him.

With a start, ʿAbdullāh realizes that day has come. The Qāʾim (ʿaj) is the new Imām.

All the weariness that had numbed ʿAbdullāh's mind vanishes at once. He looks again at the house and is surprised to see the guards whispering to each other. Using the gathering darkness as a cover, ʿAbdullāh inches closer to the house to hear what they are saying. He is only able to make out a few words:

"... house thoroughly searched...only the mother...no sign of the child...khalīfah...angry..."

That is all ʿAbdullāh needs to hear. He backs away into the shadows, satisfied.

Imām ʿAskarī (ʿa) had explained that this would happen. It was all part of Allah's plan to foil Muʿtamid's plots, since the evil Abbasid khalīfah was determined to kill both Imām ʿAskarī (ʿa) and his heir. To protect the young Qāʾim (ʿaj) from those who wanted to harm him, Allah would make him go into hiding. During this first phase of his absence, only very few companions would know where he was.

But out of sight did not mean out of reach. Imām ʿAskarī (ʿa) had made this clear. He said there would be a system in place to allow communication between the Shīʿah and their Imām (ʿaj). They would not be stranded without a leader.

Remembering all this fills ʿAbdullāh with hope again. The connection is not broken. All he needs to do is find the missing link that will help bridge the gap between him and his new Imām (ʿaj).

Early the next morning, ʿAbdullāh visits the friend who helped him arrange secret meetings with Imām ʿAskarī (ʿa) on his trips to Samarra. There, with the help of the Wikālah, a hidden network of the Imāms' most trusted companions that has developed over the decades to manage the affairs of the Shīʿah, he learns how he can reach Imām Mahdī (ʿaj). He can go to the special representative, or deputy, who has been appointed to meet the needs of the Shīʾah community during the Imām's absence, known as the nāʾib. He learns that the first nāʾib is ʿUthmān ibn Saʿīd al-ʿAmrī, a close companion of the ninth, tenth, and eleventh Imāms (ʿa). He also finds out that ʿUthmān has moved his base to Baghdad in order to keep a safe distance between himself and the ʿAbbasid rulers in Samarra.

Armed with this knowledge, ʿAbdullāh sits down to write a letter to his Imām (ʿaj). He lays out a piece of parchment, dips his quill in ink, and begins to write:

In the name of Allah, the All-Beneficent, the All-Merciful

Salāmun ʿalaykum O grandson of Allah's Messenger!

Please accept my condolences for the martyrdom of your father. When I was lost, he helped light my way. Without him, and without your grandfather, Imām Hādī (ʿa), I would not be who I am today.

After your father's martyrdom, I was devastated. I couldn't stop thinking about what we had lost as a Muslim ummah. But then I remembered seeing you on my last visit before your father's martyrdom, and I remembered what he told me about Allah's plan for your future. You gave me hope.

These days are difficult for your Shīʿah, and we are still in pain. If you could share something with us—something to reassure us, to inspire us, to guide us—it would help us bear these trials patiently and give us strength to prepare for your return.

Was salām

Your faithful servant, ʿAbdullāh

As soon as the ink is dry, ʿAbdullāh sets off for Baghdad to meet with the nāʾib, ʿUthmān ibn Saʿīd.

After meeting with ʿUthman and entrusting him with the letter, ʿAbdullāh waits for the young Imām's reply. He decides that once the reply comes, his quest to find the missing link is complete, and that he can return to his family with a new sense of hope and purpose.

When ʿAbdullāh returns home to his family in Qom, it is a bittersweet reunion. They try to smile as they hug and greet each other, fighting back tears until they can fight the tears no more. Then they hug each other all over again, and this time their shoulders shake with sobs as they grieve together for the loss of Imām ʿAskarī (ʿa).

After sharing his family's grief, ʿAbdullāh shares with them his ray of hope. He explains the situation of their new Imām (ʿaj) and then produces the letter. They all gather around to read the words of the Imām of their time (ʿaj):

In the name of Allah, the All-Beneficent, the All-Merciful

Salāmun ʿalaykum dearest ʿAbdullāh,

I also remember meeting you one time when you were visiting my father. He always spoke very highly of you. It is good to hear from you, and I pray you and your family are doing well.

I want you to know that I fully understand your pain. When my Shīʿah suffer, I suffer. Your pain is my pain. But we can take comfort in knowing that Allah is in charge of our affairs and that He will guide us to what is best in the end. Our job is to do what we can to the best of our ability, have patience, and trust in Allah.

I'd like to share with you a ziyārah that you can recite whenever hard times make you feel desperate and hopeless, like now. Inshā'Allāh it will bring you closer to Allah, His representatives, and His guides. When you send us your salāms through this ziyārah, know that we hear you and send you our salāms in return.

Was salām

On a second page, in the Imām's elegant handwriting, is a ziyārah that begins with the words that will come to be known as Ziyārat Āl Yāsīn.[1]

سَلاَمٌ عَلَىٰ آلِ يٰسٓ
اَلسَّلاَمُ عَلَيْكَ يَا دَاعِيَ ٱللَّهِ

Peace be upon the family of Yāsīn
Peace be upon you, O caller toward Allah

ʿAbdullāh kisses the letter and the ziyārah and hugs them to his chest. His family crowds around him, smiling through their tears. This time, they don't have to fight them back because they are tears of joy.

1 This can be found in the Kisa Publications book An Illustrated Ziyarah Guide to Iraq; it can also be found on duas.org.

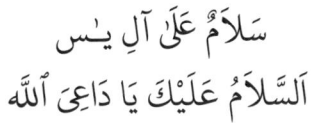

Epilogue

ʿAbdullāh lived during Imām Mahdī's minor occultation, known as the ghaybah ṣughrā. During this time, Imām Mahdī (ʿaj) appointed four deputies, known as the nuwwāb, one after another, as his special representatives. When the Shīʿah wanted to communicate with Imām Mahdī (ʿaj) and ask him questions, they could send letters to him through the nāʾib, who had direct contact with him. In this way, ʿAbdullāh was able to contact the Imam (ʿaj) through ʿUthmān ibn Saʿīd, the first of the four.

The names of the others were Muḥammad ibn ʿUthmān ibn Saʿīd al-ʿAmrī, Ḥusayn ibn Rūḥ, and ʿAlī ibn Muḥammad as-Samurī. Each nāʾib, in turn, appointed his own representatives to the various cities and regions of the Muslim world. ʿAbdullāh became one of ʿUthmān's representatives in Qom and continued to serve during the time of Muḥammad ibn ʿUthmān as well.

Today, we live in the major occultation, known as the ghaybah kubrā. We no longer have a nāʾib with direct access to Imām Mahdī (ʿaj), but we still have systems in place that help us connect with the Imāms (ʿa).

For over two and a half centuries, the Imāms (ʿa) worked tirelessly to train their followers for the ghaybah. Thanks to them, as Shīʿah, we have been able to build a tradition of scholarship that is firmly grounded in their teachings. ʿAbdullāh played his own part in building this tradition. He compiled ḥadīth and wrote books on theology, the concept of Imāmah, the ghaybah, as well as other sciences. One of his most important collections of ḥadīth is called Qurb al-Isnād. Today, we can look to our fuqahāʾ—expert scholars who have dedicated their lives to deriving Islamic law from Qurʾān and ḥadīth—so that we can know what Allah wants from us. This system is called taqlīd.

But that isn't all. We can still build a personal relationship with our Imāms (ʿa), especially the Imām of our time (ʿaj). We have opportunities to remember them on special occasions throughout the year. We can call out to them through duʿā and ziyārah. We can ask for their help and intercession on the Day of Judgment. Allah has given them the power to see and hear us, even if we can't see and hear them.

There are times when the Imāms (ʿa) seem so far away, but we can get closer to them. What we need to do is find those missing links that will bring us together, such as the scholars who help us understand what they have taught us. Then, we'll realize those links were never missing. They were there all along—just hidden from our view.

CHAPTER 21

Two Promises and a Miracle

Qāsim ibn Aʿlā

At 100 years old, Qāsim ibn A'lā still doesn't have a child. His secret wish and constant prayer is that Allah will one day grant him a son. A lifetime of waiting has taught him to be patient and to never lose hope in Allah's generosity. He is inspired by the stories of Prophet Ibrāhīm ('a) and Prophet Zakariyyā ('a), who were both granted sons in their old age, out of Allah's grace. Following the example of these great Prophets, he is content with Allah's decree, whatever it may be, and he keeps praying.

Qāsim's faith gives him strength and energy that make him seem much younger than he really is. When the people of Azerbaijan look at him, they don't see a 100-year-old man. Instead, they see a man who works day and night to solve their problems—a man whose source of guidance and inspiration is Imām Mahdī ('aj).

The people turn to Qāsim for answers. He will gladly sit and talk with them for hours, listen to their troubles and questions, and give them advice where it is needed. Since the time of Imām Hādī ('a), he has acted as a representative of the Imāms (ʿa) in this region. Even now, during the ghaybah, he is in touch with Imām Mahdī (ʿaj). He can directly contact the Imām's nāʾib and send his letters through a special messenger. At the end of these letters, he includes some of the questions he was not able to answer and asks for additional guidance. He always finishes by reaffirming his pledge of allegiance to the Imām of his time (ʿaj):

Master, I am with you until my dying breath. Inshāʿ Allāh, when I die, I die fighting for your cause.

One evening, as Qāsim is just about to roll up a finished letter, he has an idea. Maybe his duʿā needs a step stool to help it reach Allah. Maybe he needs to give it wings so that it can fly. Of course, Allah hears all prayers, but He encourages His servants to use certain avenues to reach Him. Qāsim knows there are some extra special people whose duʿās are always answered, and Imām Mahdī (ʿaj) is one of them. Maybe, if he asks the Imām (ʿaj) to pray for him, Allah will grant Qāsim a son.

The more Qāsim considers the idea, the more excited he gets. Since the Imām (ʿaj) is so close to Allah, his duʿās are always accepted. He is free of any sins that might act as a barrier between him and his Lord. And, if it turns out that

Qāsim's lifelong wish is not the best thing for him after all, the Imām ('aj) can guide him toward something even better. After this train of thoughts races through Qāsim's mind, he sees that there is still some space left at the end of the letter. So, he dips his quill in ink and humbly writes out his request.

Although weeks pass before Qāsim receives the Imām's reply, the wait is nothing compared to the 100 years he has already waited. When he and his wife read the letter together, they see, in the Imām's handwriting, the promise of a child soon to be born. They read the line over and over again until tears roll down their cheeks and blot the page:

Qāsim, Allah will soon reward your patience and your prayers with the son you and your wife have longed for. I pray he follows in the footsteps of his parents and fills your lives with joy.

Within the year, their son is born. Qāsim thanks Allah for fulfilling this promise. In honor of Imām Mahdī's martyred father, Qāsim names his child Ḥasan.

As the years pass, Qāsim's age begins to catch up to him. He feels it in his bones. But he is at peace. Every time he glances at his son, his heart brims with love and pride. He is content. He is happy. He knows he can rely on his son, who has become a source of comfort for him in his old age.

By the time Ḥasan is a young man, Qāsim begins to notice that his son's face is slightly blurred around the edges. Week by week, the world becomes dimmer and dimmer. He realizes that his eyes are failing him. One day, Qāsim wakes up and opens his eyes, but cannot see. He sits, blinking in the darkness—blind.

Qāsim accepts his loss of sight without complaint. He was blessed with clear vision for over a century. Even now, he possesses a clearer spiritual vision than most people who enjoy the use of their eyes. He reminds himself of the plight of Prophet Yaʿqūb (ʿa) who lost both his eyesight and his son, and he is forever grateful that he has a son like Ḥasan by his side.

Life goes on for Qāsim. He finds meaning in everything he does because he does it all for Allah's sake. He can still talk with people around him and help guide them like he used to. He is able to spend more time in worship than before. And now, he can bask in the pleasure of hearing his son's voice—talking to him, reading to him. Qāsim knows that he can't possibly thank Allah enough for filling his life with such blessings.

One afternoon, Ḥasan hurries into the room where his father is resting with a letter in his hand.

"Father," he says, putting his hand on Qāsim's shoulder, "A messenger came with a letter for you. Do you want me to read it for you?"

"Thank you, Ḥasan," Qāsim says, lightly touching the hand on his shoulder. "Yes, please do."

Ḥasan takes one glance at the letter after opening it and looks up at his father, his eyes shining. He takes his father's hand and gently places it on the signature at the bottom of the page. "It is a letter from our Imām," he whispers excitedly.

Tears fill Qāsim's milky, unseeing eyes. "A letter from my master," he murmurs to himself, "Alḥamdulillāh. But I can't read it."

"I'll read it for you. Don't worry," Ḥasan says, wiping his father's tears. "I'll help you follow along with your finger. Even if you can't see the words, you can still feel them with your finger—and your heart."

Qāsim takes a deep breath. He isn't complaining. Instead of dwelling on his loss, he tries to conjure up an image of the Imām's handwriting in his mind's eye to make up for what he is unable to see now. It occurs to Qāsim that he has never seen Imām Mahdī's face. He searches his memory for a glimpse of Imām ʿAskarī (ʿa) and wonders how closely Imām Mahdī's features would resemble those of his noble father.

As Ḥasan begins to read the first lines of the letter, Qāsim feels a sudden urge to raise the letter to his forehead and touch it to his eyes. Ḥasan watches in amazement as his father blinks to clear the tears from his eyes and meets his son's gaze.

"Am I dreaming?" Qāsim gasps, disoriented for a second. "Ḥasan, my son…I can see you!"

"Father!" Ḥasan exclaims, awed by the miracle unfolding before him. "Truly, the Imām's words are filled with blessing!"

"Alḥamdulillāh," Qāsim murmurs, seeing the letter for the first time. "Now we can read it together."

Together, father and son read the letter from the Imām (ʿaj). Both their faces are bright with joy until they reach the letter's end:

…Qāsim, you have served your community with compassion and sincerity for more than a lifetime. I am proud to have a companion like you. You have earned my pleasure and Allah's pleasure in this world and the next. Qāsim, in 40 days, the Angel of Death will come visit you and take you on a journey from which you will not return. Don't be afraid; you are well-prepared for this journey. Let your loved ones know so that they can prepare for your departure. Let them know that I will be praying for them, and for you.

Was salām

Now it is Ḥasan's turn to weep. He throws his arms around his father and sobs.

"Will you really be leaving us in 40 days?" he asks in a broken voice.

"It is Allah's will," Qāsim says in a comforting tone. "It is part of His plan for me. He has decided that my life is complete. Alḥamdulillāh, I have lived a long life, and during that time, I was able to serve my Imām and...and raise a wonderful son like you."

Qāsim's voice wavers for a moment. "Ḥasan, not everyone is blessed with such a long life or the same opportunity to serve. Not everyone is blessed with such a son. And not everyone is blessed with a warning before death comes. Ḥasan, let's thank Allah for these blessings, and let's make the most of our time together. Allah has given us time to prepare. Let's use it in a way that will make Him happy."

They sit together in silence for a while before Qāsim speaks again. "Ḥasan—more important than anything else is your faith in Allah and your loyalty to your Imām. After making sure your faith is strong, you need to do your best to help others do the same. Can I entrust you with the task of guiding those around you to the truth and helping them also stay loyal to the Imām of our time?"

Ḥasan looks up at his father's wrinkled face: his wispy white hair and snowy white beard, his forehead knobbly with many long sajdahs, his eyes like two bright stars peeking past the clouds that had covered them up for so long.

"I will do my best," he says. "I will try to help the people the same way you have helped them for so long. But I will miss you."

When the sun rises the next morning, Qāsim is still on his prayer mat, the same spot he has been all night long. He has spent the night thanking Allah and praying for those around him: his family, the Shīʿah, the Imām (ʿaj).

He has 40 days to prepare for his transition from this world to the next. Instead of sitting back and counting down the days, Qāsim is determined to make the most of every last second he has on this earth. Not everyone is granted the gift of knowing when they will die, so he does not want to waste Allah's gift. He quickly dresses himself and goes toward the bazaar to take care of some unfinished business.

The people are astonished to see Qāsim stride confidently into the bazaar. When he says his salāms, he makes eye contact with people, nods his head, and smiles. They gaze wonderingly at their beloved elder, who by some miracle, has regained his sight overnight.

One man in particular watches Qāsim closely from the shadow of his shop. His name is ʿAbd ar-Raḥmān. Though he is many years younger than Qāsim, he is still an elder of the community, as well as a friend. He waits until Qāsim is within earshot, and then calls out to him.

"Salāmun ʿalaykum, Shaykh Qāsim! Alḥamdulillāh, you've grown younger since I last saw you! Come, let's talk for a little while. Has something happened recently that I don't know about?"

Qāsim doesn't respond immediately. The unfortunate truth is that ʿAbd ar-Raḥmān has always doubted the existence of Imām Mahdī (ʿaj). Since the news he has to share is from

Imām Mahdī (ʿaj), Qāsim is afraid that his friend will take it lightly and perhaps refuse to believe in it. In the end, Qāsim decides it's worth trying one last time.

"ʿAbd ar-Raḥmān," he says, weighing his words carefully. "It has to do with the Imām of our time."

ʿAbd ar-Raḥmān's warm smile turns chilly and skeptical. "Are you going to tell me, again, that I'm supposed to believe in this invisible Mahdī who you claim is alive even though nobody can see him? Are you going to show me another letter and ask me to accept it as proof of his existence? Don't waste your breath trying to convince me. I can't believe what I can't see."

But Qāsim doesn't give up that easily. He holds up the letter in his hand. "You're right. I do have another letter from our Imām—just like the letter I received almost twenty years ago in which he gave me the good news of a son. If you've ever seen my son Ḥasan, you'll know that promise came true. When I touched this piece of paper from the 'invisible Mahdī' to my eyes, I could see again. Look into my eyes. Do you see the proof that you're looking for there? In the letter, our Imām has told me that I will die within 40 days. Starting today, count down the days. If, by the end of 40 days, I am gone, then you will know that the Imām truly has knowledge of the unseen and that he is real. Tell me, if this promise proves to be true, will you believe? Will you believe in your Imām?"

ʿAbd ar-Raḥmān is speechless. "I…I don't know," he mumbles.

Qāsim's voice softens. "In case it *is* true, let me say my farewells. We may not see each other again." The two friends embrace, and Qāsim continues on his way, hoping that his words will help guide his friend before it's too late.

Within a few weeks, Qāsim comes down with a high fever and can no longer leave his bed. He knows that the Imām (ʿaj) never lies and that the end of his time on Earth is near.

On the 40th day after receiving the Imām's letter, Qāsim's family gathers around his bed, weeping. They are all startled when he slowly sits up and begins to speak, his voice faint, but steady. One by one, he sends his sālams on each of the Maʿṣūmīn and turns to face the direction of each one's burial site. When he reaches the name of Imām Mahdī (ʿaj), he closes his eyes, and his face lights up with a radiant smile. Then, his body relaxes, his head falls back onto his pillow, and he lies still.

When the sounds of mourning in the streets reach ʿAbd ar-Raḥmān in his home, he knows, without even having to check, that it is the 40th day. He no longer tries to resist what his heart and his mind have been trying to tell him all along. The promise in the letter holds true. He can't deny any longer that the Imām (ʿaj) is real.

He is suddenly overwhelmed with a flood of emotions: grief at the death of his friend and mentor, shame at his stubborn denial of the truth for so many years, and an uplifting sense of hope and purpose that comes with renewed faith.

He realizes that it was Qāsim's solid faith that kept his heart and soul so young. It was Qāsim's faith that prepared him to meet his Lord. As he grows older, ʿAbd ar-Raḥman sees that faith makes life richer and sweeter, and he prays that, when his time comes, he will also be ready.

CHAPTER 22

Ḥusayn's Mission

Ḥusayn ibn Rūḥ an-Nawbakhtī

It is evening, only a few minutes before Maghrib. Dusk has just begun to cover Baghdad like a velvety dark blanket. Just as he is preparing to do wuḍūʾ, Ḥusayn hears an urgent knocking at his door.

The door opens to reveal Jaʿfar, one of Ḥusayn's close friends. His face is creased with worry.

"Salāmun ʿalaykum, Ḥusayn," he says, speaking hurriedly. "I know it's late, but I had to come right away. You know that Muḥammad ibn ʿUthmān, the nāʾib of the Imām, has been sick for a few weeks. His condition has suddenly gotten much worse. I don't think he is going to survive the night. He has sent for you; he said he wants to speak with you. We don't have much time—will you come with me?"

"Wa ʿalaykum salām—yes, of course," Ḥusayn says, quickly grabbing his cloak. "I'm ready; we can go."

When Ḥusayn and Jaʿfar enter the home of Muḥammad ibn ʿUthmān, there are eight other men gathered around the sickbed. The ailing deputy's body convulses with painful coughing. But despite being very weak, he manages to smile as his two companions join the others and kneel by his bedside.

At the moment, Muḥammad is one of the only people with direct access to Imām Mahdī (ʿaj). He is the second nāʾib, or deputy, of the Imām (ʿaj). The first nāʾib was his father, ʿUthmān ibn Saʿīd, who had been a close companion of the 9th, 10th, and 11th Imāms (ʿa). When his father passed away, Muḥammad was appointed to fill his place.

Throughout his life, he has had the Imām's complete trust. Now, as life fades from his body, it is time for Muḥammad to announce Imām Mahdī's choice for the next deputy. He clasps Ḥusayn's hand and opens his mouth to speak, but he is overcome by a fit of coughing. Jaʿfar quickly pours water into a bowl and passes it to Ḥusayn, who helps the dying deputy take a few sips.

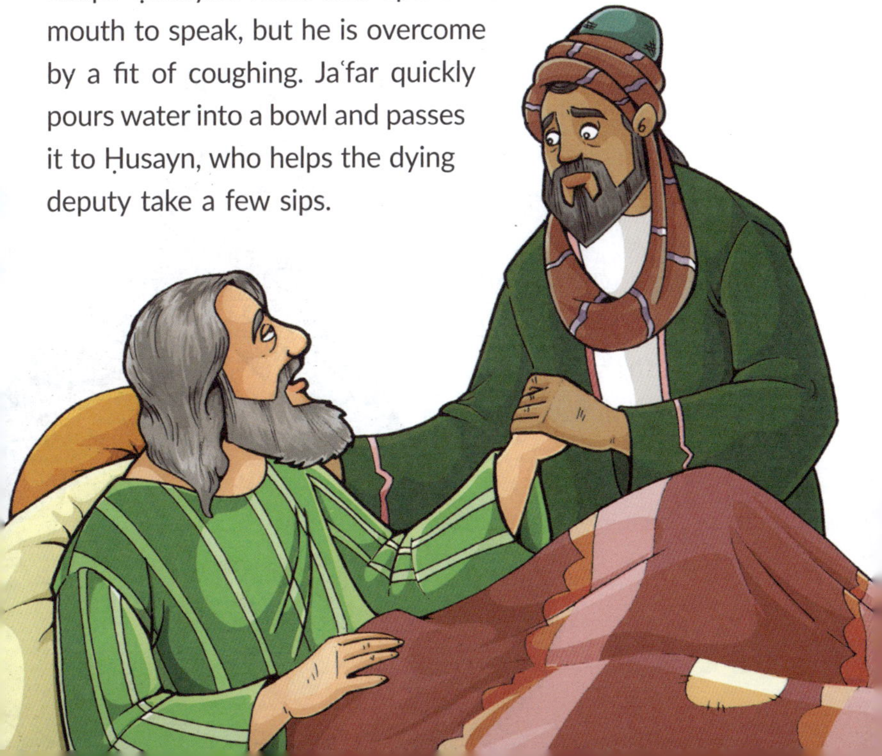

"Ḥusayn," Muḥammad rasps, his voice hoarse, "I must tell you…something…very important. It is my…duty…to announce…the next deputy. Our Imām has chosen…you… for this position." He tries to sit up and reach for something but is forced to lie back down. "Look under…my pillow," he manages to say. "There is…a letter."

Ḥusayn carefully slides the letter out from where Muḥammad had placed it for safekeeping. He opens it and sees that it is a letter from Imām Mahdī (ʿaj) to Muḥammad. The end of the letter is about him:

…I trust Ḥusayn ibn Rūḥ to carry on your mission. He is honest and faithful. I know he will serve the Shīʿah to the best of his ability. Please convey this message to him along with my warm salāms. I pray Allah gives him the strength to overcome whatever challenges stand in his way…

The rest of the letter contains details for how Ḥusayn can contact the Imām (ʿaj), and what his new responsibilities are. Ḥusayn kisses the letter, his eyes brimming with tears. He is honored that the Imām (ʿaj) has trusted him to be the main connection between the Shīʿah and their master. But it is a position that comes with enormous responsibility. He prays that his intentions remain sincere and that he does not stray from the right path. He prays that he lives up to the Imām's expectations and that he fulfills this new role in the best possible way.

A weak, whispery cough makes Ḥusayn turn his attention back to Muḥammad. The old man's breathing is harsh and uneven, and he is struggling to say something. Ḥusayn is barely able to make out the words of the shahādah before Muḥammad's soul reunites with its Creator:

"I testify that there is no god except Allah, that Muḥammad is His Messenger, and that ʿAlī is the rightful successor."

For most people, it is no surprise that Ḥusayn ibn Rūḥ is the nāʾib after Muḥammd ibn ʿUthmān. From a very young age, he served as part of an underground organization of companions called the Wikālah that was established by the

Imāms (ʿa) to help manage the affairs of the Shīʿah. During Muḥammad's time as a nāʾib, he acted as a link between the nāʾib and other leaders among the Shīʿah. Muḥammad always spoke highly of Ḥusayn, and the people always respected Ḥusayn for his good character.

However, there are some people who doubt his appointment. They claim that he was chosen as the next nāʾib because he was good friends with Muḥammad ibn ʿUthmān, not because he actually deserves the position. With time, the majority of these people come to realize that these accusations are false, and that Ḥusayn was directly appointed as the nāʾib by the Imam (ʿaj) because of his virtue and loyalty.

In the ghaybah ṣughrā, or minor occultation, he is the lifeline that connects the people to their source of guidance and inspiration: Imām Mahdī (ʿaj). They look to him to resolve their doubts, and when he is not able to give them an answer of his own, he turns to Imām Mahdī (ʿaj) for help. In this way, he makes sure the Shīʿah know that their Imām (ʿaj) cares about them deeply, even though he is hidden from view.

By the time he becomes the Imām's deputy, Ḥusayn's reputation has reached even the palaces of the khalīfah, Muqtadir ʿAbbās. The khalīfah's ministers admire Ḥusayn's leadership skills and often ask for his opinion. Indirectly,

Ḥusayn sometimes has a say in how the government runs things, and he does what he can to resist the khalīfah's attempts to make life difficult for the followers of the Imāms (ʿa). He communicates with his allies in the government and encourages them to help the Shīʿah get into government positions. The goal of this strategy is to gather useful information about the current state of the Abbasid government while offering different forms of relief to the rest of the Shīʿah community.

Of course, the khalīfah's respect means nothing to Ḥusayn. Whatever he does, he does for the sake of the Imam (ʿaj) and the Shīʿah. For Ḥusayn, serving a ruler who does not fear Allah can never be a source of pride for a self-respecting Muslim. Being Imām Mahdī's deputy is an infinitely greater honor. His true loyalties lie with the Imām (ʿaj), not with the false khalīfah. He knows that he will be in trouble if the khalīfah ever finds out, but he decides that he would much rather risk the khalīfah's anger and serve Imām Mahdī (ʿaj) than enjoy an important government position and abandon the Imām (ʿaj).

As the attitude of the Abbasid leaders changes, there are times when the government is more hostile toward the Shīʿah, and there are times when it is less hostile. Sometimes, Ḥusayn is forced to act in secret to avoid persecution. Then, for a short while, conditions improve, and he is able to do his job openly again.

However, when some groups among the Shīʾah try to rise up against the government without the guidance of the Imām (ʿaj), Ḥusayn ends up being blamed for supporting these uprisings. As a result, the Abbasid government arrests him and throws him into prison.

Ḥusayn spends five long years in a dimly lit cell, with nothing to drink but lukewarm water and nothing to eat but stale bread. He is cut off from the outside world, trapped in darkness. But he is not discouraged. From the beginning, he has known that his role would come with its own hardships and challenges. He knows that the enemies of the Ahl al-Bayt (ʿa) will continue to do everything in their power to make the Shīʿah suffer. If his time in prison is Allah's way of testing his loyalty to Imām Mahdī (ʿaj), then he wants to make sure he passes this test. When he feels loneliness creep over him, he remembers that Allah is watching over him. When he feels suffocated by the gloom, he remembers the plight of past Imāms (ʿa) who also suffered in prison at the hands of wicked rulers. These thoughts give him comfort and strength when coarse bread and water fail to do so.

After five years, Ḥusayn's steady patience pays off. Some of the new ministers in top government positions are Ḥusayn's blood relations. They share a common ancestor known as Nawbakht. Because of this connection, the new ministers use their influence to help Ḥusayn and reduce government oppression of the Shīʿah. At long last, the Shīʿah are able to breathe again, and Ḥusayn is able to resume his duties without having to fear for his life.

Despite Ḥusayn's dedication to the community, and despite the fact that he has Imām Mahdī's complete trust, some of the Shīʿah doubt him from time to time. With the Imām (ʿaj) in the ghaybah, communication is limited. Doubts and questions naturally arise—not only about Ḥusayn, but sometimes even about Imām Mahdī (ʿaj) himself. One of Ḥusayn's main roles as a nāʾib is to resolve these doubts and prevent further confusion and division. So, instead of feeling offended, Ḥusayn confronts these claims with patience and dignity. He sees them as another trial, another test of faith. No one said his path as the Imām's deputy would be easy.

One day, a man named Muḥammad ibn Ibrāhīm approaches Ḥusayn to ask him a question.

"Was Ḥusayn ibn ʿAlī the Imām and vicegerent (walī) of Allah during his time?" he asks. "Was his killer an enemy of Allah?"

Ḥusayn replies, "Yes, of course. Both of those statements are true."

Muḥammad looks uncertain. "But why would Allah allow His enemy to kill His vicegerent? How is something like that even possible?" It is clear that Ḥusayn's reply is difficult for him to process.

Sensing Muḥammad's confusion, Ḥusayn continues, "It is true, without a doubt, that Allah is All-Powerful, and He has control over all of creation. If He wished, He could have stopped Yazīd from killing His walī. However, in His infinite wisdom, He gave humans free will. Instead of forcing us all to obey Him, He gives us the ability to choose right from wrong. This is how He tests us and sees what our hearts are made out of. On the Day of Judgment, we will see whether we have passed or failed that test. Yazīd failed the test, and he will be punished most severely.

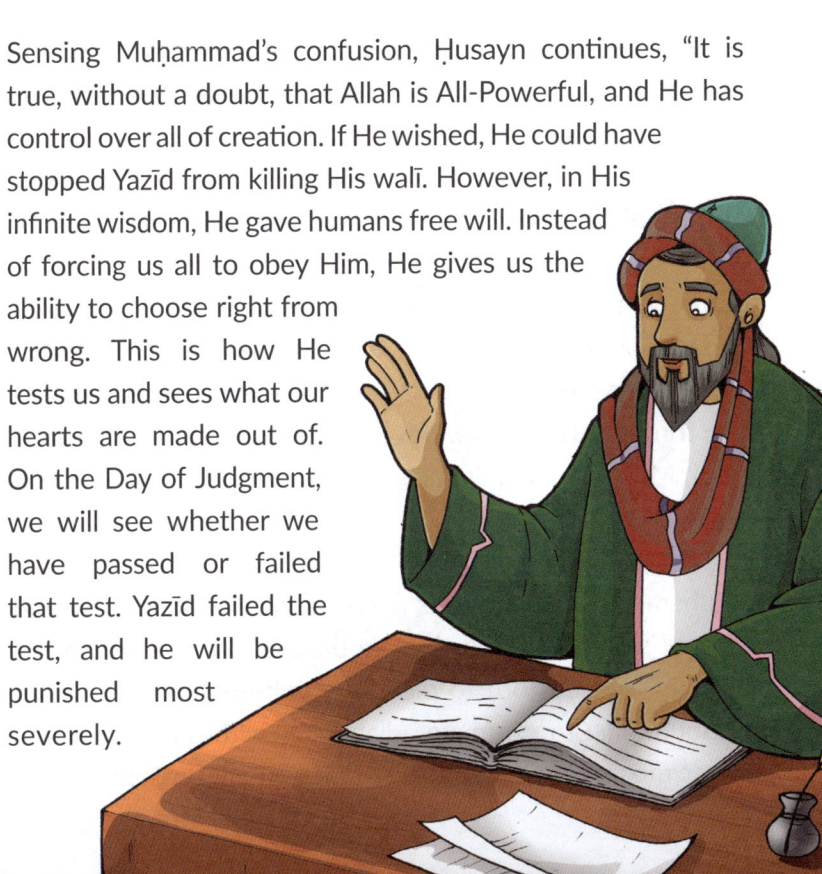

Imām Ḥusayn (ʿa), on the other hand, will be rewarded with the greatest blessings imaginable. Justice will be served in the end."

Muḥammad isn't convinced by Ḥusayn's explanation. Instead of admitting that he still doesn't understand, he begins to doubt Ḥusayn's authority.

"How can we be sure that what you say is true?" he demands. "How can we trust that you speak on behalf of the Imām? How can we know that you're not just spreading lies?"

At this point, Ḥusayn can tell that Muḥammad isn't speaking out of hatred, but out of frustration. He sees that the man before him loves Imām Ḥusayn (ʿa) and is struggling to understand the reason for his death. Instead of trying to give him an even more detailed reply, Ḥusayn tries to connect with him through their shared love for the Imāms (ʿa). If he can't reach Muḥammad's mind, maybe he can touch Muḥammad's heart.

"Muḥammad," he says, his voice quiet, but firm, "I would rather be thrown to Earth from the sky, die of thirst in the hot sun, and be torn to pieces by vultures before I would attribute a lie to my Imām. Allah is my witness that I would never mix my words with the words of the Imām."

When Muḥammad sees the intensity of Ḥusayn's loyalty, he falls silent. He realizes that he was wrong to doubt Imām Mahdī's deputy. He and Ḥusayn love and serve the same master. That shared love forms a powerful bond of trust.

As Muḥammad walks away, his confidence in the Imām's deputy restored, Ḥusayn thinks about the fate of the Imām after whom he was named. Allah gave Imām Ḥusayn (ʿa) the mission of standing up against evil. Even though that divine mission meant certain death, Imām Ḥusayn (ʿa) never wavered, not once. He stayed strong and stood his ground. In the end, he succeeded in opening the eyes of the Muslim ummah to the tyranny of Yazīd, and he and his companions achieved the highest station in Paradise.

Ḥusayn prays to Allah that he can be as courageous as his namesake. He prays that he can fulfill the mission he has been given with the same patience and resolve with which Imām Ḥusayn (ʿa) carried out his mission.

In all his 21 years of serving as Imām Mahdī's deputy, Ḥusayn never meets Imām Mahdī (ʿaj) without wearing some subtle, sweet-smelling perfume. He knows it is the sunnah of the Prophet (ṣ) and the Imāms (ʿa) to use perfume, and he wants to honor this tradition.

After his death, his family buries him in a section of the graveyard that is near his favorite perfume shop so that his fragrance can mingle with all the other lovely scents that fill the air whenever anyone walks in to buy perfume.

CHAPTER 23

The Power of Duʿā

ʿAlī ibn Bābawayh

A man lies in sajdah in a candlelit room, deep in prayer. Tears stream down his face and pool around his turbah as he whispers to his Lord. He whispers thanks, begs for forgiveness, and asks Allah to grant him his needs between one ṣalawāt and another.

"My Lord, You have the treasures of the Heavens and the Earth. To give is easy for You, while I am nothing without Your gifts. Hear my prayer, O Hearer of Your servant's cries!"

The people of Qom know him as ʿAlī ibn Bābawayh, a great and knowledgeable scholar. Everyone comes to him with their questions and seeks his advice. But when alone with his Lord, he knows how humble his status is before the greatness and might of Allah.

His head bowed in humility, ʿAlī thinks, *Maybe the mistakes that I have made are blocking my duʿās from reaching Allah. Maybe I should ask him for my needs through someone he loves very much, someone who is already very close to him...*

A part of a letter he had received from Imām Askari (ʿa) several years ago, before the Imām's martyrdom, floats to the surface of his mind:

Dearest 'Alī! Ready yourself for the reappearance of my son, the Qā'im. That is the best deed our ummah is capable of doing. He is the one through whom Allah will answer all our prayers. Was salām.

These words give him comfort, and they remind him that there is no one on Earth closer to Allah than the Imāms ('a). If he takes his request to the Imām of his time, the Imām ('aj) can pray for his needs before Allah.

Even though Imām Mahdī ('aj) is in the ghaybah, it is still possible to contact him through his special deputy, or nā'ib, Ḥusayn ibn Rūḥ. 'Alī decides it's time to travel to Baghdad and pay Ḥusayn a visit.

Over the next few days, 'Alī prepares for his journey so he can meet with Ḥusayn ibn Rūḥ. As the nā'ib, Ḥusayn connects the Shī'ah to their Imām. People come to him with their questions, and he takes their questions to the Imām ('aj) himself in order to learn the answers. Just as so many people look to 'Alī for advice because they know his knowledge is greater than theirs, he decides to turn to Imām Mahdī ('aj) in his time of need, humble and sincere.

In the presence of the nāʾib, ʿAlī is silent as he gathers his thoughts.

Ḥusayn smiles and says, "It's good to see you, ʿAlī. Tell me, what is new in Iran?" ʿAlī replies in detail about the people of Qom, the questions they ask him, and the problems that he notices in his community.

Once he is finished, ʿAlī reaches into his travel bag, pulls out a stack of letters, and holds them out for Ḥusayn to take.

"These letters include some of the questions people have asked me that I haven't been able to fully answer, along with some of my own questions. When you meet with the Imām, please convey my salāms to him."

But Ḥusayn does not take the letters right away. Instead, he asks, "Tell me about your family. Is your wife well? Your children?" ʿAlī pauses before replying, surprised that the nāʾib already seems to know what is on his mind.

"My wife is well, alḥamdulillāh, but we have no children. This is why I have come to you. I am grateful for all that Allah has given me, and I know that He knows what is best for me. Sometimes I wonder, if, in His wisdom, Allah has decided that it is best for us to remain as we are, without children… " He trails off.

"ʿAlī, you know the door of duʿā is always open," Ḥusayn says gently. "Never doubt the power of prayer. Ask your needs of Allah. He listens to every prayer, and He answers every prayer, though not always how you expect it. And know that you are not the only one who prays for your well being and success. There is always a prayer on the lips of our Imām for the well being and success of his Shīʿah."

ʿAlī feels encouraged by Ḥusayn's advice. He decides to go ahead and ask for the Imām (ʿaj) to pray on his behalf. He requests some parchment and a pen and begins to write. Once finished, he tucks among the many scrolls this sincere and heartfelt note:

In the name of Allah, the All-Beneficent, the All-Merciful

Salāmun ʿalaykum, O grandson of the Messenger of Allah!

Each day, I try to follow in your footsteps, and I know your high station before Allah. Because of this, I have a small request to ask of you. My wife and I have no children. We dearly wish that Allah grant us a child who will continue your mission of spreading knowledge and understanding of Islam. Please, remember us in your prayers. We are forever grateful for all that you and your family have done for us.

Was salām,

ʿAlī ibn Bābawayh

After giving his bundle of letters to Ḥusayn ibn Rūḥ for safekeeping, ʿAlī turns to embrace him one last time. "Thank you for reminding me of the power of duʿā," he says. "Thank you for reminding me of my Imām."

Several months pass. ʿAlī and his wife wait patiently for a reply. During the day, they carry out their duties to Allah and the people around them with care and compassion; during the night, they persist in prayer and supplication. Never once do they pause in praising and thanking Allah. Never once do they forget Him. Every step of the way, they work to please Him and prepare for Imām Mahdi (ʿaj) through strengthening their faith and performing good deeds. At long last, their patience and persistence is rewarded with the Imām's reply:

Your prayers have been accepted. Allah will soon grant you two sons. May they grow to bring joy to the hearts of their father and mother and earn Allah's pleasure by serving Islam.

Tears well up in ʿAlī's eyes. He falls prostrate in sajdah out of gratitude to Allah and prays for Allah to shower the Imām (ʿaj) with health and wellbeing and every manner of blessing. Then, he and his wife embrace as they smile and laugh and weep and thank Allah over and over again for fulfilling their cherished dream.

By trusting in Allah and turning to Him for help, they achieve the greatest happiness imaginable.

Epilogue

Within a few years of each other, the two sons are born from the duʿā of Imām Mahdī (ʿaj): Muḥammad and Ḥusayn. ʿAlī spends the rest of his years raising his sons and guiding his people. His family flourishes as a household of knowledge, learning, and wisdom.

Early one spring morning, he passes away and is buried near Sayyidah Maʿṣūmah's sacred shrine.

His sons carry his legacy onwards. Both Muḥammad and Ḥusayn become great jurists. Muḥammad ascends to the highest tiers of scholarship in the footsteps of his father.

When he becomes older, he writes several books, many of which are among the most important books in Shīʿah literature. We know him today as Shaykh Ṣadūq.

Through their humility, compassion, love for their Imāms, and dedicated service to Islam, ʿAlī and his family earn a lofty rank in the eyes of Allah. They are a role model for all Shīʿah who want to follow in their footsteps and hope to share in that same reward.

Glossary

Abbasids: A dynasty of rulers after the Umayyad dynasty; descendants of ʿAbbās (the Prophet's (ṣ) uncle), who usurped the government

Adhān: The call to prayer

Ahl al-Bayt: Divinely appointed family members of Prophet Muḥammad (ṣ)

Akhlāq: Islamic morals and ethics

Alḥamdulillāh: All praise is for God

Allah: The Arabic term for God, a culmination of all His names and titles

Allāhu Akbar: God (Allah) is Greater than anything the mind can imagine

(The day of) ʿArafah: The 9th of Dhul Ḥijjah, when the rituals of the Ḥajj pilgrimage begin

(The plains of) ʿArafāt: An area east of Mecca where

pilgrims spend the 9th of Dhul Ḥijjah (the day of ʿArafah) in worship and reflection

ʿAṣr: The obligatory afternoon prayer

Āyatullāh: A term of reverence used for Islamic scholars who have attained the highest levels of scholarship

Bāligh(ah): An individual who has come of age and is responsible for his or her deeds

Bismillāh: (I begin) in the name of God

Dhikr: Remembrance of God (Allah)

Dhul Ḥijjah: The 12th month of the Islamic calendar in which Ḥajj is performed

Duʿā: Supplication; a way in which we call out to God and establish a connection with Him

Duʿā at-Tawassul: A supplication in which we ask the 14 Maʿṣūmīn to intercede with God on our behalf

Fajr: The obligatory morning prayer

Fuqahāʾ (sing. faqīh): Jurists; scholars who are experts in deriving Islamic law from sources such as the Qurʾān and ḥadīth

Ghaybah: A period of occultation in which Imām al-Mahdī (ʿaj) is hidden away as part of God's plan

Ghaybat al-Kubrā: The major occultation; the second phase of Imām al-Mahdī's absence that continues to this day

Ghaybat aṣ-Ṣughrā: The minor occultation; the first phase of Imām al-Mahdī's absence in which a few special companions were able to communicate with him

Ḥadīth: A report or narration from the Prophet (ṣ) or Imāms (ʿa) that include sayings and actions

Ḥajj: A pilgrimage to Mecca performed in the 12th Islamic month that is obligatory on every Muslim once in his/her lifetime if certain conditions are met

Ḥaram:A sacred mausoleum, usually in which an Imām or important personality is buried; also used to refer to Masjid al-Ḥarām in Mecca

Imām: A divinely appointed leader; can also refer to the leader of congregational prayer or a community leader

Imām ʿAlī (ʿa): The 1st divinely appointed leader; his name means the exalted

Imām Ḥasan (ʿa): The 2nd divinely appointed leader; his name means good

Imām Ḥusayn (ʿa): The 3rd divinely appointed leader; his name means good

Imām as-Sajjād (ʿa): The 4th divinely appointed leader; his name means the one who frequently does sajdah (prostration)

Imām Muḥammad al-Bāqir (ʿa): The 5th divinely appointed leader; his name means the one who uncovers knowledge

Imām Jaʿfar aṣ-Ṣādiq (ʿa): The 6th divinely appointed leader; his name means the truthful

Imām Mūsā al-Kaẓim (ʿa): The 7th divinely appointed leader; his name means the one who swallows his anger

Imām ʿAlī ar-Riḍā (ʿa): The 8th divinely appointed leader; his name means the one who earned God's pleasure

Imām Muḥamma al-Jawād (ʿa): The 9th divinely appointed leader; his name means the generous one

Imām ʿAlī al-Hādī (ʿa): The 10th divinely appointed leader; his name means the guide

Imām al-ʿAskarī (ʿa): The 11th divinely appointed leader; his name means the one exiled to ʿAskar in Samarra

Imām al-Mahdī (ʿaj): The 12th and final divinely appointed leader; his name means the guided one

Imāmah: Belief in the 12 Imāms (ʿa) as divinely appointed spiritual leaders and guides after Prophet Muḥammad (ṣ)

Injīl: The Evangel, the holy book revealed to Prophet Jesus on which the modern Bible is partly based

Inshāʾ Allāh: God-willing

ʿIshāʾ: The obligatory night prayer

Islam: The religion of complete submission to Allah governed by divine laws

Jamarāt: The three pillars that represent Shayṭān at **Mina;** pilgrims stone them as part of the rituals of Ḥajj; today, the three pillars are now one wall

Jamarat al-ʿAqabah: The largest of the three Jamarāt

Jannah: Paradise

Jannat al-Baqīʿ: Graveyard in Medina near the Prophet's grave where four Imāms and many great companions are buried

Kaʿbah: The cube-shaped building situated in Mecca, at the center of Masjid al-Ḥarām; its foundations were laid by Prophet Adam (ʿa), and it was rebuilt by Prophet Ibrāhīm (ʿa) and Prophet Ismāʿīl (ʿa) at the command of Allah; it is also the direction faced in prayer (the qiblah)

Kafan: Burial shroud

Khalīfah (Caliph): Vicegerent or successor; refers to the Prophets as vicegerents of God and to the successors of Prophets; however, commonly used to refer to political leaders, such as Abbasid and Umayyad rulers who usurped the right to rule from the Prophet's family

Khums: A charitable tax on certain windfalls and savings that is equal to one fifth of one's annual savings

Khuṭbah: A short sermon or speech

Kunyah: A way of referring to somebody as the father of, son of, mother of, or daughter of someone else; it is used to show respect or endearment

Maghrib: The obligatory evening prayer

Maqām Ibrāhīm: The stone on which Prophet Ibrāhīm (ʿa) stood when he was building the Kaʿbah; his footprints are miraculously imbedded in it

Marwah: One of the two mountains in Mecca next to the Kaʿbah between which Hājar ran when searching for water; this practice (saʿy) is now part of the rituals of Ḥajj

Masjid: Mosque

Masjid al-Ḥarām: The Sacred Mosque; the sanctuary that surrounds the Kaʿbah

Maʿṣūm(īn): One(s) who is (are) inerrant (free of all sins, flaws, and impurities) through the divine protection and knowledge of God

Miḥrāb: The prayer niche at the front of a masjid that indicates the direction of the Kaʿbah in Mecca (the qiblah)

Minbar: Pulpit

Muʾadhdhin: The one who gives the call to prayer (the adhān)

Muslim: One who follows Islam and submits completely to God

Nāʾib (plu. nuwwāb): A deputy, specifically of Imām al-Mahdī (ʿaj) during his ghaybah

Qāʾim: A title of Imām al-Mahdī (ʿaj) that means one who will rise up

Qurʾān: The holy book of Muslims that was revealed to Prophet Muḥammad (ṣ)

Rakʿah: One unit of prayer

Rukūʿ: The act of bowing down in prayer

Ṣadaqah: Optional charity

Ṣafā: One of the two mountains in Mecca next to the Kaʿbah between which Hājar ran when searching for water; this practice (saʿy) is now part of the rites of Ḥajj

Sajdah: Prostration

Ṣalāh: Prayer

Salāms: Greeting of peace that Muslims exchange when they meet one another; also used when ending prayer

Salāmun ʿalaykum: Peace be upon you

Ṣalāt al-Layl: The (optional recommended) night prayer

Ṣalawāt: An invocation of blessings on the Prophet (ṣ) and his Ahl al-Bayt

Saʿy: One of the rites of Ḥajj; walking back and forth between the mountains Ṣafā and Marwah

Sayyid(ah): Title of respect for descendants of the Prophet (ṣ)

Shahādah: Declaration of faith that consists of bearing witness that there is no god but Allah, and Prophet Muḥammad is His Messenger

Shahīd: A martyr; someone killed in the way of Allah

Shaykh: A title for a respected scholar or elder

(Graveyard of the) Shaykhayn: A famous graveyard in Qom near the shrine of Lady Maʿṣūmah

Shayṭān: Satan

Shīʿah: Those who follow Imām ʿAlī (ʿa) and the Imāms after him in obedience to the order of Allah and His Prophet

Sunnah: The practice of the Prophet (ṣ) or Imāms (ʿa)

Sūrah: A chapter of the Qurʿān

Takbīr: To say Allāhu Akbar (God (Allah) is Greater than anything you can imagine)

Taqlīd: The practice of referring to the most qualified jurist in order to find out Islamic legal duties

Taqwā: God-consciousness

Tashahhud: A statement similar to the shahādah, the declaration of faith, that is recited in prayer

Ṭawāf: One of the rituals of Ḥajj; circumambulation around the Kaʿbah

Turbah: A clay tablet upon which Shīʿah place their forehead in sajdah

Umayyads: The dynasty of rulers from the descendants of Umayyah who usurped the Caliphate from the household of the Prophet

Ummah: A group of people united by their beliefs

ʿUmrah: An optional pilgrimage to Mecca that can be performed almost any time of the year

Wa ʿalaykum salām: And peace be upon you, too

Walī: Guardian

Was salām: An alternate form of saying salām, often used to close a conversation or letter

Wikālah: A network of companions/agents established by Imām aṣ-Ṣādiq (ʿa) and expanded by later Imāms that allowed them to manage the affairs of the Shīʿah; this allowed them to perform their religious duties, as well as